HENRY COOPER
H FOR 'ENRY
MORE THAN JUST AN AUTOBIOGRAPHY

HENRY COOPER
H FOR 'ENRY
MORE THAN JUST AN AUTOBIOGRAPHY

RETRO CLASSICS

RETRO CLASSICS
is a collection of facsimile reproductions
of popular bestsellers from the 1980s and 1990s

H for 'Enry was first published in 1984 by Willow Books

Re-issued in 2012 as a Retro Classic
by G2 Entertainment
in association with Lennard Publishing
Windmill Cottage
Mackerye End
Harpenden
Hertfordshire
AL5 5DR

Copyright © Henry Cooper 1984

ISBN 978-1-909040-35-9

Produced by Lennard Books
a division of
Lennard Associates Limited

Editor Michael Leitch
Designed by David Pocknell's Company Ltd

Printed and bound by Lightning Source

This book is a facsimile reproduction of the first edition of
H for 'Enry which was a bestseller in 1984. No attempt has been made
to alter any of the wording with the benefit of hindsight, or
to update the book in any way.

CONTENTS

The Man Who Gave Up Russian Dancing 6
Taking Stock 14
Adventures With The Bishop 24
Take Fifty-Six 44
One At A Time, Ladies 64
Confessions Of A Golf Celeb 74
Charity Begins At Hendon 86
The Fight Report 102
Me And My Italians 115
Walking The Dog 122
What Next? 126

THE MAN WHO GAVE UP RUSSIAN DANCING

By the time I was thirty-seven I was starting to get these messages. It was nothing sudden, just a little warning every so often, but they all pointed to the same conclusion: my pay-days in boxing were getting into the very low numbers. At best, if I was sensible, I had a couple more fights left in me, and probably just the one. Jim Wicks, my manager, had noticed these signs also, but he didn't say anything and for months we never discussed it. All the same, I knew that he knew, and that one day we would get round to putting it into words.

What kind of messages? Well, there's the one you get when you're in training for a fight, and the sparring partners you've hired to knock down stay on their feet. At one time we hired up to five sparring partners for the final two-week build-up to a fight. We paid them good money, £20 a round, which was more than they would earn from an ordinary fight, and for that money they knew they had to work hard. I didn't pull my punches in the gym and even with the sixteen-ounce gloves and the headguards I reckoned I would be knocking out a couple of the fellers, so they wouldn't last the fortnight. That wasn't happening any more. Sure, I might hurt them, and maybe knock them down, but not so they didn't want to know any more.

Part of it was the timing, which wasn't working like it used to, but the main part was the trouble I was having to get to proper peak fitness. Now, when I went into the gym it would take three days for the muscles to get good and supple. But if, in that time, I over-reached or pulled a muscle, it would take a week or more for the stiffness and soreness to go away. It's not all that surprising. Anyone who can see forty on the horizon is lucky if they aren't collecting a few aches and pains from just doing the ordinary things they do at home and in the garden and in their work. In my case, I was in my seventeenth year as a pro boxer and I knew enough about my body to see that parts of it were wearing out.

At one time I could do Russian dancing – just like those

THE MAN WHO GAVE UP RUSSIAN DANCING

Russians in the old Cossack costumes, shooting out their legs in time to the music. I used to do it as an exercise. One day I was in the gym and we had some press and visitors there. I was giving them the Russian dance act when suddenly – Yaah! – I'd torn the cartilage in my right knee. That needed an operation, followed by a fortnight's complete rest, followed by a long period of struggle to get back my fitness. I had lost two inches on my thigh muscle girth with the wasting, and it took nearly four months before I was strong again. During

most of that time I was training every day, Monday to Friday, with the Arsenal squad, either at Highbury or at their training ground at London Colney. That was in 1969, and the injury cost me my European title which I had to give up because I wasn't fit to defend it within the six months required by the European Boxing Union. Something else I gave up was Russian dancing!

I also had elbow trouble. This went back to when I was a kid just out of school. I used to work for a building firm as a roofer and tiler's mate. One day the bloke in charge of me wanted a chimney cowl and he sent me down to a builder's yard to get one. I went on my bike, and on the way back I was pedalling along with this great heavy thing on my shoulder when the wind caught it and off I came. As I fell I banged my left elbow and chipped a piece off the bone. At Lewisham Hospital they couldn't do any more than bandage it up; they told me to come back in three or four months when I would have got to the top of their waiting list and they would make a proper job of it. But I was young and busy and I forgot about it. The elbow was stiff for a time and then that wore off, so I left it.

The trouble was, the chips that had come off the bone were still in the arm, and over the years they worked themselves into the elbow joint. With the use I was putting the arm to, the chips were being ground down to powder and then dispersed in the bloodstream. All this grinding process was putting a lot of extra wear and tear on the elbow, and eventually I had it X-rayed and went to see Sir William Tucker, the orthopaedic surgeon who looked after the Queen and did Churchill's kneecap. I was twenty-six at the time, and he told me that my left elbow had the wear of a man in his late seventies. So I could expect trouble from it every so often for as long as I stayed in boxing. Over the last two or three years of my career Tucker's predictions came more and more painfully true. After a fight, the left arm used to lock up solid and for two or three days, being a left-hander, I couldn't comb my hair, pull on a shirt, or do anything that meant flexing the elbow.

THE MAN WHO GAVE UP RUSSIAN DANCING

This may sound a right groggy picture – the portrait of a boxer on his last legs, his last arms, last everything. Strangely enough, though, the year before I retired was a very successful one. In March 1970 I took back my British and Commonwealth titles which I had given up the year before in protest against the British Boxing Board of Control's refusal to let me fight Jimmy Ellis for the WBA world title, largely because the WBA were the 'wrong' side; they, the British Board, preferred to give their support to the New York Commission which operated the rival WBC titles. As a result, the British title had passed to Jack Bodell, and on the night, although he was craftier and less clumsy than he had been at our last meeting, I outpointed him fairly comfortably. That was my first fight after the cartilage operation, the knee held up well, and Jim Wicks and I felt that we should challenge for the European title which I had surrendered because of the knee and which was now in the hands of Jose Urtain, a Spanish slugger from the Basque country with a sideline in championship rock lifting – one of the local sports out there. We met in November 1970, after promoter Harry Levene had given himself a few extra white hairs chasing Urtain all over Spain to get his signature. The fight was at Wembley, my best venue. Early on, Urtain swung and missed a lot but caught me with one which opened a small cut but wasn't serious. For the rest of the fight I gave my left arm a good workout jabbing it into Urtain's face until his eye was so swollen that the referee stopped it at the end of the eighth round.

So, where was I? In theory I could have gone in again for the world title. Had it still been Ellis, we might have fixed something, but the champion now was Joe Frazier and Jim Wicks would never have let me take up an offer that involved mixing it with Smokin' Joe. Frazier, like Sonny Liston, was a slugger with a difference. He was heavy – two stone more than me – he was rough, always coming forward with dangerous punches, giving you no let-up, brushing your best shots aside, wearing you down for the killer blow. A box-fighter like Ellis would have been a good possibility, but the dividend from a last pay-day with Frazier was something that Jim refused to allow. This meant that at world level I was out of contention until the title passed to someone with a more compatible style.

At home the new challenger was Joe Bugner, then aged twenty-one and getting a lot of build-up as the new Golden Boy. We signed to meet at Wembley on 16 March 1971. At stake were my British, European and Commonwealth heavyweight titles. For Bugner it was a clear-cut issue: he was the up-and-coming lad, sixteen years younger than me, two or three inches taller, a stone and a half heavier. If he won, he was well placed in two or three years to take on the world. He had a lot going for him, and a lot to chase after. As for me, I wanted one more thing out of boxing: to win the fight and retire as the undefeated champion.

The decision to retire had crept up on us over the months. Training for the Bugner fight was the kind of chore I had grown to expect. I could still do it, but that didn't mean I had to go on doing it for ever. Anyway, in boxing there is no 'for ever'. When Jim and I got round to discussing it, the main decision was already fixed in our heads and it was more a question of looking at what we might do next. Jim was optimistic that there was room for a new career developing the PR and sponsoring work that already kept us busy for quite a lot of the time between fights. About two weeks before the Bugner fight I was talking on the phone to my wife, Albina, and I found myself saying to her that this one really was the last. She said: 'Thank God for that.' Although she had always supported me in what she accepted was my work, Albina had no love for boxing. I knew that she had been waiting four years for me to tell her that I was going to pack it in, because that was the last time we had discussed it. She had been marvellously patient. As she once said: 'Whatever Henry's done he's done it himself. I've only been able to help by not nagging.'

The day came and we went to Wembley. The records tell that I lost the fight, and the three titles, by a quarter of a point. I was more than convinced that I had done enough to win, and so was the crowd of 10,000 who took the verdict in not very good heart and booed, stamped and pulled out some of their choicest abuse. To judge from the expressions on their faces, the people in Bugner's corner were also convinced that I had won. They couldn't believe it when they were given the victory. All the important observers were equally sure that I had taken the fight – all except one. Unfortunately, he was Harry Gibbs, and Harry Gibbs was the referee. And that, under British rules, was that. It hardly needs saying that I was totally choked at the time, but I had no intention of making a big protest out of it. Not so Jim Wicks,

'...it was lucky for both of them that my brother George (that's him on the left) was near enough to grab Jim and hold him back.'

who was all for getting straight over to Harry Gibbs and landing one on him there and then; it was lucky for both of them that my brother George was near enough to grab Jim and hold him back. Jim was more angry than I had ever seen him, before or since.

There was nothing for it but to cut the quickest possible route through all the clamouring Pressmen and fans, go home, unwind and get a good night's sleep. Next day would be soon enough to see what a future completely outside boxing had to offer.

TAKING STOCK

I woke up on the morning of 17 March 1971. The house was still there, Albina was still there. I could hear the boys – Henry Marco and John Pietro – making the sort of racket that all boys seem to need to kick up as their way of starting a new day. 'Oh well,' I thought, pulling the eyes open, 'there's only one thing that's different this morning. I'm not a boxer any more.'

'Eh?' said a voice from inside my head.

'That's right,' another voice answered. 'Not a boxer any more.'

That was enough to start a conversation.

'Blimey, that's quick,' said the first voice. 'Last night I was a boxer, and for twenty-seven years before that. What am I going to do now?'

'All the other things you are doing already,' said the second voice. 'The advertising and the personal appearances. You just carry on like before. Don't worry. Go and look in your diary. You're not idle, you know.'

'No, that's true. But it won't be the same, will it?'

'It may not be exactly the same. It can't be exactly the same, can it, because you aren't fighting any more. So the best thing you can do is to try and find out what it *is* going to be like.'

'How do I do that?'

'You could get out of bed for a start.'

It was certainly true that my retirement from boxing was not an open-and-shut case like you get when you retire at the end of your working life. I did have other work to be getting on with, and that would keep things going at least for a while; plus I had earned a fair amount from boxing, and although the tax man had snatched back a good three-quarters of it, I had still been able to invest some of what remained. Through Jim Wicks and Harry Levene I had met an insurance broker called Charles St George and I became a director of two of his companies. I had also put up some money and joined an underwriting syndicate at Lloyds. This syndicate specialized in marine insurance, so if a big shipping accident hit the news I was dashing to the phone to find out if my group was involved.

The main part of my other work was making personal appearances, opening shops and so on, and being a guest on radio and television programmes. I was also involved with *A Question of Sport*, and had already done three series as one of the team captains.

In a radio programme which was broadcast in 1971, I described a typical week at that stage in my life. It began on the Monday morning with a trip to Broadcasting House in a BBC car to appear as a guest on Pete Murray's record programme. Later I met Jim Wicks for lunch at Simpson's in the Strand to go over any new offers he had received, and he told me there was a new supermarket which they had asked me to open. Next day I flew up to Newcastle from Heathrow on the midday plane to open the new township at Killingworth which had been built by Costain's. That evening I had dinner with the mayor, chief of police and other civic high-ups at the Gosforth Hotel, and in the morning we went out to do the opening and have lunch. Then I flew back to London and was home by eight-thirty. On Thursday morning I had a golf lesson at my club, Ealing, and then I played in a four-ball.

On the Friday I went to Sheekey's fish restaurant to meet Jim Wicks and Frank Butler of the *News of the World* who wanted to chat over lunch about an article he was doing on young boxers. After lunch I met Albina and we went down to the Italian club in Clerkenwell, the Mazzini Garibaldi, where we are members and Albina can keep in touch with the Italian community (all rabbiting away in a language I still haven't got to grips with, but that's another story).

Saturday morning was free, then in the afternoon I opened a fete in Wembley – a local affair – and in the evening it was on with the black tie and down to the Savoy for a charity ball. Next day I was up early to catch a train to Manchester to record two episodes of *A Question of Sport*.

That made a nice mixture of work, travel and

relaxation, with me doing my best to be entertaining when it was needed. Fortunately, this is something that has never come hard to me. Anyone who has done well in a sport – whether it's boxing, football, cricket or whatever – needs to realize nowadays that he *is* an entertainer. It's no good just doing your thing and trying to scoot off home before anyone catches up with you. Few sportspeople would quarrel with that nowadays because in the last decade there has been a big boom in companies sponsoring events, and in sports stars endorsing equipment and clothing for playing in, doing keep-fit, jogging and so on. If what I read on my Corn Flakes packet is anything to go by, people are even dressing up in special gear at breakfast time to do exercises in front of their TV sets!

    Sport has become a big industry, and I reckon that the professionals should really see themselves as belonging to a part of showbiz. In 1971 most people didn't have quite that outlook, but I decided early on that most boxers were basically show-offs and so the trick was to develop a bit of style and then go along with it and enjoy yourself.

    Looking at that sample week I have just described, some people might think I was busy enough anyway, without looking for more work. If they were really nosey, they might say: 'Look. He must have got so much for doing the Pete Murray, this from Costain's, this from *A Question of Sport* – plus all the other perks and bits in between. Blimey, what's he doing worrying about the future when he's got it made already?'

    Well, I will admit that even in those days I had my share of luck in the way a lot of interesting jobs kept coming along, and for the time being I could feel reasonably secure despite the fact that I knew the big fight purses were a thing of the past. Even so, you don't get exactly rich on BBC fees for a quick guest appearance, nor do you cop all that much for doing a half-hour show. The out-and-out commercial work commands bigger fees, but then don't forget that I was also fitting in a fair amount of charitable work as well. So, while I have never been one to bite any hand that wants to feed me, when I first retired I was well aware that I was in the position

TAKING STOCK

'ENRY, HOW MUCH DO YOU 'COP' FOR DOING THIS HALF HOUR SHOW?

of someone who has started a business and just about got it off the ground all right, but now I had to build on it and expand it. After all, it only needed a couple of doors to suddenly shut and I would have felt the draught – no question.

All boxers have these niggling worries when the time comes to stop fighting, and they have all heard a few stories – mainly from what you might call the 'bad old days' – of fighters who never made a go of it financially, or who got themselves into trouble, or who tried to make a comeback into boxing and mucked it, or who just went straight downhill and out of sight because the ring was the only trade they could cope with. Things are a lot better nowadays, mainly because people are better educated and more worldly about the business side of things, and more willing to consult bank managers, accountants and solicitors before they make an important decision about their future.

Some retired boxers do extremely well. If you take it from the top, you only need to look as far as the Walkers – George and Billy – to find a very well-heeled set-up. The Brent Walker company built Brent Cross, they put up hotels all over the place, in Arabia and Egypt for instance, plus they have interests in cinemas, film production, and all kinds of other projects. Another boxer from my day who has done very well is Dave Charnley, the former lightweight champion. He went into building and land speculation and he is now a very wealthy boy. From more recent times, Jim Watt is doing very well. You also find a lot of boxers who may not have been great names in their ring days but who then went into business and have made possibly a bigger success out of their second careers. One who comes to mind is Teddy Haynes, who was in our stable. He was Midland middleweight champion. Now he's got two pubs down the Old Kent Road. He's got the Henry Cooper (which is very nice for me) and the Prince of Wales. Joe Lucy, who was British lightweight champion when I turned pro, is another who is doing well in the pub business. He's got a big place in West Ham which is more like a club, running discos and dances and all that kind of thing.

So, without making this into a catalogue of fighters who have made a good living after they stopped boxing, I want to make the point that most do manage to make the switch without too much difficulty. You get the odd exception, the occasional hard luck story, but you get those in any walk of life. Also, in the old days it was generally much harder to make a successful break from boxing because a lot of the lads were fighting for peanuts, so they never had a chance to put anything aside for the future.

The licensed trade has attracted quite a few ex-boxers, but I never felt the pull of that kind of life for myself. I like to get out and about, travel and do my PR work wherever the bookings come up. Even if I could have had the best pub in London (however you judge that), I wouldn't have liked to be tied down there all day and most of the night, doing more or less the same thing all year round. I would say this about the restaurant business also – although I suppose it would be all right to have an interest in a restaurant and just go in a couple of times a week to meet and greet people. Beyond that, I wouldn't want to be involved. I know from Albina, and the years she spent at Peter Mario's, that running a restaurant means a lot of headaches. Albina was part of the family who owned the place – it was her Aunt Maria, Peter Rizzi's wife, who brought her over from Italy. So she knows from first hand about the constant problems of finding and keeping good chefs, good waiters, and all the everyday hassles that a restaurant owner has to try and deal with quietly without the customers seeing.

Mind you, on an ideal level I could have had quite a decent family restaurant. Albina's two brothers, Giovanni and Marco, could have been the chefs, her brother-in-law runs a restaurant so he could have been the maître d', with Albina and Teresa, her sister, as the waitresses. I reckon they'd be worth three or four crossed knives and forks in your average restaurant guide, and a few rosettes as well.

Thinking of pubs rather than restaurants, as we were a little while back, there is another drawback to being the guvnor of a pub if you were once a boxer. This probably applies more to fighters from the lower weight divisions, but Alan Rudkin told me that he gave up the pub he had in Liverpool because by closing time all the drunks were more interested in having a bundle with him than they were in drinking up. Imagine having to dodge about with a bunch of comedians like that every night of your life. I am only glad I have stayed well clear of it.

In fact I have really only had one aggro experience with a member of the public, and that happened while I was still fighting. My brother George and I had been celebrating our twenty-sixth birthday with Jim Wicks, and after the lunch we drove Jim back to his house in Eltham. I was at the wheel and we turned into Jim's street. Just ahead was a cyclist. It wasn't far to Jim's house but I reckoned there was enough space to overtake the cyclist and pull up ahead of him, so that is what I did. It was a wet and windy day and the cyclist had his head down as he pedalled along. He must have thought he still had a clear road ahead of him because the next thing I heard was a thud in the back of the car. Then I saw this man pushing his bike up towards where I sat in the driving seat. Just to be friendly, and to see what had happened, I wound down the window and poked my head out. Silly, really, because – Thwack! – this feller catches me across the mouth with a backhander. So now I'm sitting there with a fat lip. Before the feller could get really keen and dish out any more, I pushed open the door quick and climbed out. George got out as well, and he is 6 feet 2 inches and broader across the chest than me, and so did Jim Wicks who was about $17\frac{1}{2}$ stone at the time.

 We looked down at this cyclist who was about fifty years old, 4 feet 9 inches tall and about as wide as my little finger. We all said: 'You cheeky so-and-so' or something like that. But he was wild, this little geezer. He glared up at us and shouted: 'Yes, you think you're brave, don't you, just because there's three of you!'

 We thought about that for a bit, while he stood there shaking with rage and looking as if he really would have had a go if I had been on my own. Then somebody saw the funny side of it and we started laughing. That saw him off, I'm glad to say. He got on his bike and pedalled away mouthing things to himself. I still had the fat lip, of course, but I had to laugh.

 Anyway, back to 1971 and there I was still wondering what the future would bring and whether there were any other options I should be considering. As I said, the PR and advertising work was rolling in nicely, and I began to feel more and more strongly that this was the kind of second career that I should develop. It appealed to me for another reason: I would be working largely for myself and by myself – with some solid assistance from Jim Wicks, of course, who was still my business manager. The point here was that we didn't need to take on other people and have all the worries of staff, wages, premises, rent, rates and all that other stuff which can make your hair curl. Besides, I had been through all that with the fruit shop.

 Back in 1965 I had been looking around for a business interest that would still be there when I finished boxing. On holiday in Las Palmas I met up with a guy who had a greengrocery stall in Holloway and was looking at shop premises in Wembley High Road. He had a partner lined up at the time, but then he dropped out and the bloke was a bit stranded. He was still wondering whether to go ahead by himself, and not fancying the idea much, when I found myself saying: 'All right. Look, I'll come in with you. You can use my name but you'll have to run the business yourself. I'll just drop in once or twice a week to see how things are ticking over.'

He seemed very pleased with this idea, and a short while later I was signing on for one of the most expensive mistakes of my life.

For the first eighteen months or so everything went really well. Our greengrocery business could have stood comparison with any shop of its size anywhere in the country. If I went there just after a fight there would be fantastic crowds, all buying stuff as well as watching me show off to the newspaper cameras, clutching a pair of caulies and larking about. Then it began to slip a bit. I think the idea of working with a celebrity went to my partner's head. I had taken him round and introduced him to some of my friends, and then he seemed to get the idea that he was a celebrity as well, so instead of one person running the shop and the other one doing occasional promotions for it, we had a position where nobody was running the shop. By then we had concessions in two supermarkets as well, and were employing sixteen to twenty people.

Stuff began to go missing from the shop and it was all getting a bit dubious. As a result, I was soon going in there – *having* to go in there – three, four or five times a week, plus weekends as well, when I could have been out earning good money for publicity jobs, or supporting charities which is something I have always tried to allow time for.

The other guy was on a bit of a short fuse as well, and when things weren't running his way he got worse and started insulting customers so they wouldn't come in any more. People who had been regulars for about two years started walking straight past. Opposite us was a store which employed fifty or sixty women who all used to come and get their greengroceries with us. One day they stopped coming in. I asked them why. 'Oh,' they said, 'we're not coming while he's here.' And they'd tell me some story about how they'd got an earful last time they came in and they weren't putting up with that.

I couldn't blame them. In a free world you do your shopping where you find the best combination of price, goods and a nice atmosphere. It's like that old-fashioned shopkeeper's saying: 'Cleanliness and civility is our motto.' It doesn't tell you anything about the quality of the goods, but it shows a lot of understanding about the human side of how to sell things.

Towards the end of 1968 the business showed no sign of getting back on its feet, and in fact the pressure on me was getting worse. The list of creditors was growing longer, and it was me they were coming to for their money because I had the big name. Getting into debt was something I had never done before. It was completely against my upbringing, and when it happened I was really put out by it. It was the only period in my life when I lay awake at night, twisting about because I couldn't see an end to the problems.

The night before I fought Muhammad Ali for the world championship, my head hit the pillow and I was asleep in five minutes. With the shop, I was awake till two and three o'clock in the morning every night. It had to come to an end, and to protect my name from being dragged through the courts – because now the writs were being got ready – I had to cover a lot of the business debts with my own money. I was about £10,000 down when, just after Christmas 1968, I said: 'Right. That's it.' And pulled the shutters down on the whole business.

It was a hard way to learn a lesson, but when I did retire from boxing that lesson was well and truly fixed in my head. In future, others could employ me and I would work for them on short-term or longer-term arrangements, with consultancies, retainers and so forth. What I would not do was start building any more human pyramids. I wasn't cut out for that kind of thing. In future there would just be me.

TAKING STOCK

ADVENTURES WITH THE BISHOP

One person I would be seeing just as much of in retirement was Jim Wicks. We never went in much for contracts – in fact we only signed one serious contract, and that was for three years when I started with him in 1954. After that it never bothered us, even though it agitated the Boxing Board of Control. People rang Jim up and said: 'Look, Jim, officially you're no longer Henry Cooper's manager. The contract you had with him ran out six months ago, but you're still signing him for fights when you aren't officially his manager.'

Jim was quite scornful. He said to me: 'What do we want contracts for?' Eventually the Board made us get contracts drawn up and signed just so that Wicks and Cooper were in line with the rule book. But in our private book contracts were a waste of time. No-one would ever have poached me from Jim, and if Jim had packed up I would have quit boxing. That was the kind of partnership we had.

When my brother George and I joined Jim, he had a stable of successful fighters. He had Alex Buxton, the British and Empire light-heavyweight champion, Jake Tuli who was Empire bantamweight champion, and Joe Lucy the British lightweight champion. He carried on this style of management for some years, based on the gym at the Thomas a'Becket pub in the Old Kent Road, but then he began to reduce his stable by not taking on new fighters when the others retired, until I was the only fighter he was looking after. Then in 1971 we retired from boxing together.

Our relationship was not the usual one between manager and boxer. We were more like father and son, and it was perfectly natural that the partnership carried on into our other business interests. I had been doing quite a lot of commercial and personal appearance work, and people knew that if they wanted to book me for some date, the way to do it was to get in touch with Jim. And we just went on using that system.

I think it was George Whiting of the *Evening Standard* who decided that Jim, with his round chubby face and ample

ADVENTURES WITH THE BISHOP

body, would look a treat in gaiters, and he nicknamed him 'The Bishop'. After that it was hard not to think of him as a kind of bishop. He was certainly a lovable character, and very good at his job as well. Whenever I boxed as a pro, I always went into the ring thinking that with Jim in my corner I was starting with at least a 60–40 chance, no matter who I was matched against. Even after we retired from the ring, old habits still stuck. One of them was to refer to one or both of us – most of the time there was no difference – as 'we'. In the end one of the newspapermen picked it up and said: 'Yeah, they've been weeing together for twenty years.'

When we started out again in 1971, there was no shortage of people coming to us with all kinds of generous schemes that were guaranteed to make our fortune and theirs. One I remember had to do with hamburger machines, but there were several offers which followed the same pattern. It was like a play or a film in three parts. In Part One the phone rings and we get this wonderful offer – never seen anything like it, marvellous, etc, can't go wrong. Part Two is slower, because it's about the money they haven't got. In Part Three Jim, in the nicest possible way, blows them out.

'That you, Jim?' they'd say at the beginning. 'Yeah, well you don't know me yet, but you wait till you hear what me and my associates have got for Henry. Put it together right and we could make *millions*.'

'Oh, yeah, could we?' says Jim, pulling a face as he settles down to hear it.

'Yeah, Jim. Millions. Can't miss. Triffic. You've never seen a deal like it…'

They'd go on and on and Jim would hear them out, and then he'd say: 'Right, I've listened to all that. Now tell me, if it's so good, if it's such a wonderful idea, what do you want to share it with us for?'

Then it would turn out that the only thing this marvellous scheme didn't have was capital. 'Well, not much, just a few grand, Jim, so we can get the first machines bought in. Then, when it's rolling, all you've got to do is sit there and collect …'

'What,' says Jim, 'you want us to put *our* money into *your* idea? Come on, don't be boring.' And he'd put the receiver down.

After a little dust-up like that, Jim's thoughts often turned to food. 'Come on, let's get out of here,' he'd say.

Although the business that Jim and I now did was not exactly what we had done before, there was no reason why we shouldn't carry on our weekly restaurant routine which was an important part of our lives. At my family home in Bellingham we had always spent a good deal of money on food, even in the days when that meant there was little left for other things. Not that we were particularly big eaters, but Mum had found herself having to feed two professional boxers – George and me – and steak has never come that cheap.

So far as Jim Wicks was concerned, food was more than just a necessity. When he said 'Look after your stomach,' he was talking about a way of life. 'Look after your stomach and your stomach will look after you.' Steak, with salad and a few boiled potatoes, is a staple of most fighters' diets. With Jim Wicks you could expect a glass or two of red wine as well, perhaps a light Beaujolais such as a Fleurie which became one of our favourites. On the Friday before a Saturday fight he was all for us going out for a good lunch, starting with a dozen oysters and Krug champagne – which was then about five pounds ten a bottle. (One bottle never did go very far anyway.)

Jim approved of wine, and he encouraged me to get a taste for it. He thought it was good not just as something to have with a meal but as a tonic also. I used to lose weight quite rapidly when I was fighting. This was to do with my build and my not having much surplus flesh. If I went into the gym to start a new spell of training, after about a week I would be down to my fighting weight but we'd still have another three weeks to go.

Jim's answer was to make sure I kept up with the red wine, and at the Thomas a'Becket he had a special mixture which he got me to take. After training I went down into the

Signing up for a nice pay-day: me and Jim with fight promoter Harry Levene.

pub and Jim ordered me a double vintage port and Guinness. He definitely thought it was building me up but my feeling, on an empty stomach and immediately after a good workout in the gym, was that it was going to my head a lot quicker than I needed, especially by the time we were out on the street.

Quite early on in our career together, a tradition developed that we would eat in certain favourite restaurants on certain days of the week. This suited us and it suited other people who got to learn where to find us if they wanted to do some business. One day in the early part of the week we'd be at Simpson's in the Strand where the main attractions were the big joints of roast beef which they carved on the trolley, the saddles of mutton and the roast duck. Another day we'd go to Jack Isow's in Brewer Street, a favourite with Jack Solomons, where they had a lot of Jewish specialities, and if you went in there often enough Jack would have your name painted on the back of the chair. Friday's call would be at Sheekey's fish restaurant in St Martin's Court, off the Charing Cross Road, where for us the high points on the menu were oysters, jellied ells, one of their lovely main dishes like Dover sole, and a bottle or two of Krug champagne. Another restaurant on our list was, of course, Peter Mario's in Gerrard Street, run by Peter Rizzi and Albina's Aunt Maria, and where in the early days Albina herself brought us many a plateful of spaghetti bolognese and veal escalope.

While we are on the subject of food, there is one man who almost deserves a chapter in his own right: Bobby Diamond. Bobby was one of the great characters in the boxing world. As far as physique was concerned, he was the Seven Ages of Man rolled into one. He began as a fighter, an eight-stone bantamweight, and then went into management. Towards the end of his life – he was about seventy when he died – he weighed more like eighteen stone, and he owed most of that ten-stone increase to the restaurants of Soho. When I first knew him I had never seen anyone put away the stuff he could. At that time I would have said that Bobby could eat anyone under the table.

He was born in Frith Street, Soho, the son of a doctor.

H FOR 'ENRY

Like his brothers who eventually qualified in France as doctors, Bobby also set out to make his career in medicine. In France it takes six or seven years to become fully qualified, and Bobby was serious about it for eighty per cent of the course, but then a year before his final exams he gave it all up to become a professional fighter.

In his day he was a good boxer. He was matched with most of the top people around at the time. Afterwards he managed maybe as many as six world champions. Robert Cohen was certainly one, and he had the Toweel brothers as well – Vic was the more famous of the two. But while Bobby was able to make a successful career in boxing, both in the ring and outside it, as a medical man he knew there was something physically strange about him, and he also knew what it was.

He was one of those unusual people who have an enlarged stomach. This meant that he could eat and eat and eat until his stomach was so full of food, it pressed up against his heart cavity. When this happened he felt pain and knew that he shouldn't eat any more. Meanwhile, of course, before he got to that stage, he had stacked away what would be a week's rations for someone like me.

Bobby got the heavy eating habit early, and at one time was an area representative for the national eating championship of France. This was held in Paris about once a year in a big restaurant, and all the contestants got round a huge oval table. Each man had to say beforehand what he was going to eat, and how much, and then the organizers weighed the food and cooked it. One of the rules was that for every kilo of food they ate, the contestants had to drink a litre of wine.

Bobby thought he'd start by ordering three kilos of meat. When it was cooked, it was brought to the table on a platter with vegetables piled all round it, and Bobby started tucking in. He must have been hungry that day because he got off to a good start and soon he was going really well; the food was disappearing steadily off his plate, and he was topping up his glass all the time from a big litre carafe of red wine. His supporters reckoned he was in with a good chance and were starting to get excited – until they looked down the table and saw what one of the late starters was up to. This guy came in, pushed his belly under the big oval table, looked up and ordered a *stone* of meat – more than double what Bobby had asked for. They cooked it, and the guy just laid straight into it and ate the rest of the field completely under the table. So that was one title – eating champion of France – that Bobby never did get his hands on.

    These eating contests seemed to work a bit like the different weights in boxing. If people gave too much weight away, they'd be right out of their class with no hope of winning. Tommy Gibbons reckoned he could eat. He had been a light-heavyweight fighter and then he took over as landlord at the Thomas a'Becket. The word got round that Tommy was keen to test himself and we set up a match between him and Bobby, to be held at the Pinocchio restaurant in London. That was one of Bobby's better nights. He tore through his food and left poor old Tommy bloated and done for after about three Osso Bucos. From the moment Bobby picked up his napkin and tucked it in – one corner in the neck, one down his lap and the other two under his arms – there was only one man in it. Tommy was on a double belting that night because they had also agreed that the loser would pay the bill!

    Bobby was typically French in the way he loved his meat covered in rich juicy sauces. Of course, at the speed he ate, not everything landed up in his mouth. Jim Wicks once looked at Bobby at the end of a meal. Bobby was sweating a bit and there was sauce all over the place. Jim said: 'He comes in the restaurant, tucks in that napkin, all beautiful and white, and when he's finished, the napkin looks like the Union Jack.'

    At Simpson's in the Strand, where the carvers come round to the tables, and you can point out the piece of meat you want, they looked after Bobby very well, and he did his best to look after them. He always wore a waistcoat, and all the pockets were well topped up with 50p pieces which he would dole out to the various waiters and carvers. Bobby was a generous man anyway, but if you think about it he had such an appetite he actually needed the waiters to spoil him rotten or he'd end up going home starving.

If Jim rang up Simpson's to make a reservation, he only had to say that Bobby was with us and they would say: 'Right. Fine. We'll get it organized.' And they did. What happened was that the carver on Bobby's station would cut a big slice of top cut and reserve it for Bobby. Then he went round all the other carvers and collected more nice crispy bits from them. By the time the plate got to Bobby it had maybe three pounds of beautiful dark brown roast beef on it. Then they brought the potatoes. Jim would have two, I'd have two, my brother George the same (a bit like the Shredded Wheats). That left about twelve potatoes on the dish for Bobby. He ate the lot. Then came a big bowl of cabbage. The rest of us took a spoonful or two: Bobby finished it. He never let us down.

It must have been in the early Sixties that a restaurant opened in Leicester Square called The Guinea. You went in, paid a guinea, and they would let you eat as much as you wanted. Bobby thought that was heaven sent. 'Vat!' he said, 'you pay ze guinay and you eat vot you vant? Iss unbelievable!'

Well, in Bobby's case it turned out to be too good to last. He went into this paradise of a restaurant where you could fill your plate, and refill it, and refill it again, all for only twenty-one shillings. He paid his money and set about the menu, and after two days they barred him.

Bobby could speak about seven languages, and by any standards he was a talented linguist. Strangely enough, for someone who was born here, the language he spoke worst of all was English. One night we were kidding around about starting a club in Soho. This was just after the girls had been taken off the streets and people were opening these little strip clubs and pick-up joints. 'Cor!' somebody said. 'That's the business to be in.'

'That's right,' said somebody else. 'All you need is to find a nice little clubroom and you're away…'

Bobby started getting quite excited at the thought of all this. 'Yez, yez,' he suddenly said. '*You* get ze building, *I* get ze voomans!' From the way he started talking, he'd have been over in France next day, recruiting. But what we could never figure out was why, after all those years, he spoke such bad English. 'Voomans.' I ask you. With one word, Bobby could turn a tasty girl into a Belgian cyclist.

One night I boxed Brian London at Belle Vue, Manchester. Next morning we were up early to catch the 7.30 breakfast train because we had some business to do in London around midday. We got on the train and Bobby was with us. After we had been going for about two minutes, a waiter came down the aisle. Bobby waved him down and asked the obvious question: 'Ven eez breakfast?'

The waiter explained: 'Not long, sir. We just have to go down the line to —— (he mentioned another town), where we pick up a few more passengers. Then we can serve breakfast.'

'But ven?' Bobby pressed him. 'Ven is ze breakfast?'

'About half an hour, sir.'

'Vat?' cried Bobby. He could not believe it. This was terrible. It meant waiting a whole thirty minutes for his first meal of the day. 'Ugh, ugh,' went Bobby, and started flapping his hands about in despair.

I was on a table for four with Jim Wicks, my brother George and Danny Holland our trainer. Bobby sat on his own at a table for two on the opposite side of the carriage (no-one ever wanted to sit next to Bobby on a train because he'd take all the seat). Five minutes out of Manchester and Bobby started eyeing the little plastic pots of marmalade which had already been put out on the table. He couldn't help it. All of a sudden there was a spoon in his hand and the marmalade in one of the plastic pots had gone. Then he had the other one which was intended for the person sitting opposite Bobby; fortunately no-one had taken the seat.

Now he turned to our table. In front of Jim was a big stone jar of Cooper's marmalade. Naturally, Bobby asked Jim if he'd pass it over, but Jim refused.

'Now, come on Bobby. You sit there and behave yourself,' said Jim. 'You'll get your breakfast one day.'

H FOR 'ENRY

Bobby looked at Jim like he was a merciless torturer, but sooner or later the waiter did come along with a bunch of menu cards. There was quite a long list of things to eat: fruit juices, cereals, grapefruit segments, kippers, egg and bacon, boiled egg, sausages and tomato with mushrooms and potatoes – the usual full Breakfast Car choice – poached egg on toast, toast and marmalade, tea, coffee, and so on, The waiter looked at Bobby and Bobby just said: 'Yez.'

'Yes?' asked the waiter.

'Yes,' said Bobby. 'I weel 'ave eet.'

He meant he wanted the whole lot. And he wasn't joking. While he was waiting for it to arrive, he asked for some bread. We counted. We counted them in and nothing came back. He had a dozen rolls before any proper breakfast got to him. When his kippers came, they were not those dwarf filleted ones you get nowadays, they were the whole fish. Bobby had no time for fiddling about, he just crunched them up, bones and all. The bacon and egg hardy delayed him at all and in a few minutes he had chewed and swallowed his way right through the card. To those of us who knew him, it was nothing special. That's how Bobby was with food – a hundred per cent keen, every time.

Years later, Bobby was having a meal with someone in a hotel restaurant in London. He explained that he wanted to pop downstairs, so he got up and left the table. Several minutes went by and the people he was with began to wonder if there was something wrong with him. When it got to half an hour and still there was no sign of him, they thought they had better have a search in case he had been taken ill.

They went down into the Gents and called for him: 'Bobby! Bobby!'

There was no-one to be seen. Then they noticed that the door of one of the cubicles was shut. One of the fellers got down and through the gap under the door he could see Bobby's feet. It was him all right, but he wasn't saying anything, nor could they get in there to help him. In the end the hotel people had to take the door off to get Bobby out. What had happened was, Bobby had suffered a fatal heart attack inside the toilet, then he fell forwards against the door, a dead weight, literally, all eighteen stone of him.

It was a tragedy to lose him, of course. He was such a lovable character. But at least he had lasted into his seventies, which was good going when you think of all the work his insides had to do for him over the years. Also, of course, he hadn't been far from a restaurant table when his last moment arrived.

Some while back in this chapter I was explaining about the restaurant routine which Jim and I had grown into. Obviously, we went to particular restaurants because we liked their kind of food and the way they cooked it, and also because we felt at home in them. The staff looked after us, and if one or two strangers came up to say hello, well that was all right too. It was part of the business. So long as they didn't want to pull up a chair and tell us about the highlights of their amateur career as a promising lightweight.

We came across someone else who liked to do what we did. Every so often in Sheeky's, the fish restaurant, Jim and I would be there on the same day as this little white-haired man. He sat over on one side, always on his own, and we got to giving each other a wave and hello. Then one day we sent a drink over. More smiles and waving. The next time we were both in, he sent a drink over to us. Thank you very much. Your health. Good luck. All this went on for some months until the owner of the restaurant said to us:

'You know who that is, don't you? That gentleman with the white hair.'

'No. We just see him in here.'

'He's Charlie Chaplin.'

'No! Go on!'

'Yes. He lives in Switzerland, but every time he is over in London he comes and has lunch with us. Says he loves the stewed eels and the jellied eels which he can't get at home.'

That made a nice little extra to our lunchtime routine. But the main purpose of it was to be around in central London in the middle of the day. All the restaurants we liked were in Soho or the West End, and that was also the centre of the

H FOR 'ENRY

boxing business and where most of the gyms were to be found. Jack Solomons had his office in Great Windmill Street, and Harry Levene was in Wardour Street. There was a lot more boxing in those days, and you would always find a lot of people buzzing round the place.

Not that you would want to stay very long in a promoter's office. If the public image of boxing has a glamorous side, then I would say this is mainly limited to the fighters who have had success in the ring and can buy a few perks and luxuries after they have had a couple of lucrative pay-days. For the rest of the sport, words like dingy and workmanlike are more appropriate. In its daily life, and how it goes about its business, boxing has always worked on the principle that people are more important than comfort. That is not to say that managers and promotors can't earn a few bob as well and buy themselves a box or two of big cigars. That also is part of the game – a bit of personal flash to keep the press boys happy and the cameras clicking. After all, if a sport or a branch of entertainment – and there isn't much difference between the two – has no style about it, then the public wouldn't want to know and it would all fold up.

I am making a point of this because quite a few people seem to have the idea that a boxing promoter's office must be like JR's suite in *Dallas*, and that the gyms must be like one of those health clubs they keep meaning to belong to – all sweet-smelling and crammed with beautiful bodies, rubber plants everywhere, marble floors, jacuzzis and all that stuff.

Well, to start with the offices, you didn't go there unless you had to. They never tried to make them comfortable, mainly because they regarded an office as a room where you did the business and that was all it was for. At Solomons's place you wouldn't even get past the outer office if you didn't have a big rating in the fight game. Partly this must have been to discourage the hangers-on, and there would always be plenty of them if you didn't watch it. So, a good restaurant was a much better place to be if you wanted to have a talk with someone. Say a journalist wanted to do an interview with me. He would ring Jim and Jim would say

'Come and have a meal with us' and name a restaurant. Then we could spend as much time as we wanted at the table, with good food and a glass or two to help things along.

As for the gyms, they were strictly for the sharp end of the business. Some of the pro gyms in London must be among the scruffiest places on earth. Also, you could smell them half a mile away, and there was nothing sweet about that smell. Jim's place at the Thomas a'Becket in South London was a little bit removed from the others in terms of distance, though not much; but that suited us fine, especially when George and me were living at home in Bellingham. It was also handy for Jim, who lived in Eltham. Jim in fact started what is now the famous boxing tradition of the Thomas a'Becket by getting Courage's, the brewers, to let him open a boxing gym above the pub. Jim also installed himself in an office next door, and originally the gym was reserved just for his own stable of fighters.

The other gyms were almost all in West One. One of the most famous was a barracks of a place just off Cambridge Circus, run by Joe Bloom. No gym ever seemed to make money, because fighters are the world's worst for paying, so the gyms had to be run on basic, no-nonsense lines; anyone who came looking for a marble palace was in for a shock. Joe Bloom's gym attracted a lot of foreign fighters, and plenty of big names trained there. He also had a few showbiz people who went there to keep fit. But Joe didn't care who you were; if you interfered with his way of doing things, or wanted to stay late, you had no chance. You could be the world champion standing there, talking to someone in your best suit, but if it was time to close Joe would come round with his big spray gun full of disinfectant – whoosh, whoosh – and if it went all up your trouser legs and everywhere, he wasn't going to apologize. All Joe cared about was his timetable, so if it was time to get the dust down and give the place a sweep, it was rough on anyone who got in the way.

Joe's attitude said a lot about gyms and what they were really for. If you were a fighter, you didn't care what the place looked like where you did your training. What you were looking for was people – other fighters you could spar with. A chromium-plated gymnasium was no good if no-one went there. Even if a place did smell, and was nothing more than a plain old sweat shop – if managers knew they could take their boys there and get them fixed up with sparring partners, that's the place they would go to every time.

You didn't need to tell that to someone like Jim Wicks. He'd known it since about the First World War. Jim died shortly before his eighty-fifth birthday, and apart from the last eighteen months or so when he was ill, he had been a character and a big name in the boxing and entertainment world for as long as anyone could remember.

Racing was his other great sport, especially on the betting side. Many's the big name who learned the techniques of the game from Jim. People like Jack Solomons, and Sam Burns who went on to run William Hill; Jack Swift was another – it was Jim who just about taught them how to reckon bets. They all went on to become millionaires and Jim was the only one of that school who didn't turn himself into a professional punter.

Not that Jim ever lost his flair for betting. He used to put bets on that made my hair curl – and it was his money that was being put at risk, not mine. A few years ago, when a couple of hundred quid was a lot of money, I have seen him lay bets for that much as if he was buying a newspaper. He didn't mind going to three hundred, even five hundred. I have seen him win ten and fifteen thousand pounds and within a week it was all back – gone. But it never seemed to upset Jim that he could lose thousands as well as win thousands. Whatever the outcome, his expression never changed. Sometimes, after a big loss, I couldn't help myself saying: 'Look, Jim. Look what you just lost. Why don't you give...'

'Son,' Jim always said, without waiting for me to finish. 'Son, the game must be played.' That was his saying, and he never complained, no matter how much he had just said goodbye to.

For myself, I owe it to Jim that I do not bet. After seeing the things he got up to I reckoned that what I had I'd worked hard for, and I wasn't going to sling it away. I still enjoy a day at the races and go to the Derby every year. I have been over to Paris to the Arc de Triomphe race, and a friend of mine, Charles St George, who's an insurance broker, owns some nice horses. But when it comes to betting, the people I go with must think I'm a right miser.

At least Jim knew all the ins and outs of what he was doing. He had been a street bookmaker before bookmaking was a legal business. At one time, he told me, he had made himself sixty thousand pounds, which at today's prices must be the same as about half a million. He had it all under his bed, and then one day a bad patch started. Every day Jim would have to send his runner back to his house with special instructions: 'Ask the wife to give you five thousand pounds.' Next day: 'Ask the wife to give you two thousand pounds.' Then: 'Ask the wife to give you ten thousand pounds.' And so on until the whole lot, the whole sixty thousand, had vanished.

In his earlier days Jim knew some wonderful characters who liked to put a few quid on the horses. There was Dan Sullivan who used to run the Blackfriars Ring and at one time managed Len Harvey. This is going back to pre-war days, but the sums that Dan and his friends liked to put on still sound impressive today. One day Jim went down to Brighton with Dan and a feller called – I think – Charles Annan, who had a horse running there. This bloke Charles quite fancied his horse to win, but he didn't want the betting mucked up on the course by anyone getting over-excited. He mentioned this to Jim and Dan.

'Oh, don't you worry about us,' said Dan, 'we only bet in shillings anyway.'

Down on the course it was all very different. Dan went wallop with about five hundred quid on this bloke Charles's horse and naturally the odds dropped dramatically. Charles was well choked but he didn't know who to blame for it. Looking around at the people connected with his horse, he decided it must have been the jockey who had been tipped off, perhaps by the stables, and then spread the word round

A quick one with the regulars at the Thomas a'Becket, in the Old Kent Road, where Jim Wicks opened the famous fighters' gym which is on the first floor.

Ready for my 1965 bout with Johnny Prescott. With me and Jim are Danny Holland and a sparring partner.

all his mates. As he was giving a leg-up to the jockey in the paddock, he said to him: 'This is the last horse you ride for me!'

So already, before the race, he'd sacked the jockey – who was quite a well-known rider at the time. When Jim Wicks found out what had happened he had to go round and see the owner. 'Look, Charlie,' he said,' 'you've made a mistake. It wasn't the jockey and his mates doing the business on the track. You ought to know about the man who was with me, the one who said he only bet in shillings. He's the one who did it. He's one of the biggest backers in the game.'

The owner, by all accounts, was glad to know what had really happened, even if it only helped to put him on his guard for the next time he ran into Dan Sullivan. All the same, he was still too riled, or too proud, to take the jockey back. He stayed sacked.

Jim wouldn't let something like that fuss him too much. He had come up the hard way himself and he knew that you could expect to take a few steps backward for however many you took forward. Jim in fact had a great pedigree as a bookie. Before the bookies on the course were allowed to set up their stands saying 'Honest Jim Wicks' and so on, Jim used to go round and collect money off people who bet with him from the card. When it came to taking bets from the toffs, it was Jim's job to wait under the boxes while they wrapped their bets round penny coins and threw them down to him.

It was a long step forward from scampering around like that to managing the business affairs of Henry Cooper, retired fighter. Jim, by then, had perhaps done enough in his working life to deserve a bit of peaceful retirement. Unlike him, I had only been working at my career for twenty-seven years – if you include the amateur part – so I had plenty of years to look forward to and make new plans.

But for the time being Jim had no idea of packing it in. That was fine with me, so we simply carried on as before, the only difference being that I didn't have to go to the gym any more and so we had more time available to offer people.

Now, for instance, if someone rang Jim and asked if I could go and open a supermarket at eleven o'clock in the morning he could accept, whereas before I might have been training and it would have been impossible.

Financially, so long as the phone kept ringing, Jim was all right until well into his eighties because he still kept his twenty-five per cent for whatever he set up for me. In the final eighteen months, when he became ill and eventually got cancer, he obviously wasn't so bright but I tried to bung him a few quid because he wasn't getting any income from any other source. Still, he'd kept going at the top for a lot longer than most. That was how he was. 'The game,' as he put it, 'must be played.' Jim Wicks could never resist a good game.

The 'Weeing Couple' strike again – collecting our third Lonsdale Belt at the headquarters of the British Boxing Board of Control in December 1967.

TAKE FIFTY-SIX

The first television commercial I ever did was an eye-opener. I had done a fair number of panel games, so I was familiar with TV studios and talking in front of the cameras, but the way the advertising boys went about their work was something else.

This commercial was for Crown Paints, and their advertising people had worked out an elaborate script involving me, a painted door and one of those boxer's speedballs – the type that is suspended at head height and the fighter hits it about a million times a minute. The idea was to have the speedball banging into the door and coming back off it – to show that Crown Paints could stand up to any kind of a battering.

I read the script in advance and it seemed fine to me, so I got to the studio at about ten o'clock in the morning, all ready, or so I thought, for a quick bit of filming. The first thing that struck me was that nothing was ready. Ten o'clock must have been the start time for everybody else, too, because the scenery and camera people were only just beginning to set things up for filming.

When they had the speedball in position, they asked me to come over and give it a few taps to try it out. I did what they asked but the result wasn't very good. The speedball was too rigid and didn't have enough travel through the air to give them the effect they wanted.

'No, no,' they said after a couple of minutes. 'No good. It won't work like that.'

There must have been twenty-five guys in the studio, all drinking coffee and shaking their heads, and after a bit one of them said to me: 'We're going to have to try it another way. Would you like to go away and come back about twelve or twelve-thirty.'

So I went off thinking: 'Blimey, what a waste of time.' I was a complete layman, of course, but I couldn't help wondering why they hadn't put up the set earlier and got someone about my height to stand in and see if it worked.

TAKE FIFTY-SIX

When I went back two hours later, they had given up the speedball idea. Instead we filmed the commercial using one of those heavy stand-up balls on a tall spring. The whole business took the best part of a day to finish, and I wasn't out of pocket for the extra time I had spent hanging about while they changed everything. Even so, when it was over I still thought it was a funny way of working. I said to Albina: 'No wonder these commercials are so expensive!'

Anyway, I was learning. Later I got to find out a good bit more about the economics of making these short films, and the fact that a big company will book a studio for the whole day just to make sure they get the thing finished off. If they do finish early, they still want their value, so they make everybody do extra takes and just go on perfecting what they've got until they run out of studio time.

One of my most successful campaigns so far has been with Fabergé, who make the Brut range. It's not really an exaggeration to say that I had been preparing to do those commercials for about twenty years. The story goes back to my amateur days in boxing. After training I would have a bath then a rub-down to keep the muscles supple and close the pores. Usually my brother George would give me this light massage, but the problem we had in those days was to find a decent kind of lotion to put on. When we began, the choice was between White Horse oils and wintergreen liniment. After you'd had a layer of that rubbed into your skin, you put your clothes on and set off for home. By the time you were warmed up a bit, you would start to give off a funny smell, a bit like horses in a stable. It certainly wasn't good for travelling on buses with, because while you were sitting there looking innocent, the other passengers would be turning round to each other and wrinkling up their noses and saying: 'Pworrh! Where's that coming from?'

If you were the last one to have got on the bus, it didn't take long for the others to work out who was stinking to high heaven, so, as long ago as the early 1950s I spent my time on buses muttering to myself: 'When I turn pro, I'm going to get something that smells better than this.'

H FOR 'ENRY

The next stage, when it came, was to go along to Woolworth's or whoever was cheapest at the time, and buy a big plastic container of cologne. Basically this was a white spirit and it did the trick. The smell wasn't brilliant but at least it didn't excite anybody on the buses, and so that was what I settled for. Years later, after I had retired from boxing, I wrote in my autobiography about how I had used cologne after training, and someone at Fabergé must have decided that I was the right person to launch their new body lotion for men, so they got in touch.

Brut 33 Splash On was launched about ten years ago, when public attitudes were very different from what they are now. If you had gone up to the average working guy in the street and said: 'Here, I've got this new cologne for men, I'd like you to splash it on every day,' the answer would have been: 'Get out. What do you think I am, a fairy?' Since those days the whole image of men's cosmetics has changed, I suppose more people are spending money on decent bathrooms, and nowadays the working man doesn't think it strange to use cosmetics like after-shave, splash-on, talcum powder, and so on.

Brut 33 was designed as a middle-priced range – as distinct from Brut Original which was more up-market – and in the beginning it was my face and voice that Fabergé used to try and persuade the public that it wasn't stupid or effeminate to 'splash it on all over'. Luckily for them and for me, it seems to have worked. Fabergé's UK sales were up round the £11 million mark last year, and I doubt if there is a main sales outlet in our big cities that I haven't been to at least once to do in-store promotions for Fabergé products. That, of course, is the sharp end of the business, where you meet the public who have come out for a bit of entertainment and who don't mind telling you what they think – especially if you have turned up a bit late because you have been stuck in heavy traffic and they have been waiting outside in the pouring rain.

All that malarkey is a chapter by itself – in fact it's the next chapter in this book. I just mention it here because it makes such a contrast with the public image which the Fabergé company has created for itself. They are one of those de-luxe firms who succeed because they look smooth and expensive, and because they are able to encourage people that they too can have a slice of the old movie-star appeal. All they have to do is go down the chemist and invest in a few of those nice green bottles.

The de-luxe message goes all the way through the firm from the very top. In physical terms that means the top of a skyscraper in New York where George Barry, the chief executive, has his office. The first time I saw it I thought I had been shifted into another world. You step out of the lift on the top floor and go down a shadowy corridor lined with grey chamois leather. To help you find your way, three fluorescent tubes in green, yellow and orange lead you to the head man's office.

When I say 'office', that is just the nearest word in the language to describe the incredible space in which George Barry works – and lives as well, if he wants to. Inside these dream headquarters he has got a self-contained module with a bedroom and bathroom. In the main part of the office is a big electric organ and seating room for a full orchestra. George Barry is a talented musician who has composed tunes with some of the great names of showbiz, and if he suddenly wants to get a band together and try out a new idea for a tune, I suppose he has only got to punch a few buttons and in next to no time musicians will be appearing through the walls and he will have the whole thing set up and ready. It really is out of this world, like a set in a fantasy movie, and after a while it becomes impossible to say what could happen there and what couldn't. If you like, it's the magic of total luxury.

This de-luxe approach is obviously more suited to some areas of business than to others. If you were selling a range of disinfectants, for instance, you'd need to be a bit more down to earth. All the same, even in the cosmetics game nothing would come right if a lot of people weren't prepared to put in a great deal of high-pressure work. One of

H FOR 'ENRY

the most notable things about the Fabergé commercials was the time and effort that went into making them.

Filming usually began early, at eight in the morning. Then, because the company had booked a full day's studio time, we continued until all that time was used up. People not connected with the film business tell me I am on a real winner with these commercials. 'Easy,' they say. 'Course it is. How long do they last – fifteen seconds? You can't be in there more than an hour knocking that off. Money for old rope.'

It's hard to get them to believe that I leave home about seven-thirty, and that to finish a thirty-second commercial I have been there, still working, until after midnight. A thirty-second film is a long one, mind you, and it can happen that you get a shorter, easier one and after an hour or two, say by ten o'clock, you may have two or three good versions in the can. But then, because the company has booked the studio for the full day, no-one says: 'Right, let's wrap it up and go.' Instead, you film variations and little extra bits. If we had filmed it first of all with me putting on a smiling face, now we'd try it with me looking serious. Then we'd try putting a different emphasis on different words. And we'd go on doing that *all* day.

Funnily enough, that is when the mistakes creep in – and later in the year you find a clip of yourself appearing on Denis Norden's *It'll Be All Right On The Night*. I had one with David Hemery. We had got a couple of good films in the can early on in the day. Then we went on and in the middle of the afternoon we were still doing these extra bits, but by then our minds had begun to wander and suddenly we were forgetting lines that we had been speaking without a hitch since half-past eight in the morning. First David got his lines all mixed up, so he went 'Oh b———!' to the cameras and they of course picked that up. Then I called him 'Arthur'. Don't ask me why, or where Arthur came from, because I still don't know!

That happened after I had done several Fabergé commercials on my own. Then the company decided to

TAKE FIFTY-SIX

bring in other celebrities to join me. We began with Barry Sheene, then there was Harvey Smith, David Hemery and Kevin Keegan. The high point of them all was a special film called 'Henry Cooper's Christmas Party', where about twenty celebs all came into the studio. We did this in June one year. It was a baking hot day, about eighty degrees outside, but in the studio it was all done up like a proper Christmas Day party, with a tree, lights, paper chains, the lot. Then Fabergé added their own extra bit of style.

Usually if you are doing a commercial which requires you to drink something, you get a glass of coloured sugar water. Not this time. The Fabergé people had the complete works. They went round all the celebs and asked each one what their favourite drink was, and then they started dishing them out like they were on an endless conveyor belt. If someone said he liked strong German lager, that was what he got – from ten o'clock in the morning. Quite a few of the lads were on champagne. Filming got under way, refills came round, and by the time we were finished it was the happiest commercial you could have asked for. People have asked me since who was on it with me, and I can still remember a few! We had our old regulars, then we had Jimmy Tarbuck, Kenny Everett, Bobby Charlton...Anyway, whoever was there it was a real classy line-up.

You can imagine, too, that with a bunch like that there was bound to be a lot of extra joking and ad-libbing. In one scene they brought round a big tray of cream cakes and Kenny Everett picked one up and stuck it on the end of Jimmy Tarbuck's nose.

'Oh no,' said Jimmy straight away, 'I don't do impersonations.'

This kind of thing was coming up every few minutes, and Fabergé kept a lot of it in the final film because it went so well with the party atmosphere.

Another funny thing about the 'Christmas' commercial was that when I woke up that morning I was in southern Portugal. I had booked a holiday down there with the family long before I knew about the commercial. But then Fabergé added a bit extra to the budget – which must have had a lot of noughts on the end of it already. They said to me: 'Right. Can you be at Faro airport early?' I said I could, and when I turned up at just about sunrise, there on the runway was a special TAP eight-seater Lear jet. We took off, and I was the only passenger. A stewardess was there to look after me and bring on the champagne breakfast. It was quite a nice way to start the day. At Heathrow they had a car waiting for me. I was rushed through customs and got to the studio at the same time as the others.

After the commercial was finished, we were all well merry but I still had a bit of travelling to do. Back to Heathrow. The jet was waiting and off I went to Faro. I got back to where I was staying that night, and next morning I was on the first tee at nine o'clock! I wouldn't want to do it every day, but it felt a bit stylish at the time.

Most of the Fabergé commercials were filmed in the studio, but some sequences had to be done outdoors. For one of these I went with David Hemery and the film crew to a nice quiet part of the country where we were able to stop the traffic and do our filming down a leafy lane. The script had me on a bike and David Hemery running along and hurdling barriers when we came to a stretch of road works. To film this, the crew had the camera mounted on a special motorized buggy. This was all right for a few takes, but then the motor broke down and all they could do was tie a rope to the front of the buggy and get all the technicians to run along towing it – like one of those naval gun crews at the Royal Tournament. The trouble was, the buggy had no brake on it so if the crew pulled it too fast or too slow, the focus was all wrong – plus, by the end of the day's filming, I have never seen a film crew so completely knackered. It was no sweat for David and me, of course; we only had our bit of action from the script to worry about. So we had to try not to laugh too much in front of the camera boys.

Another sort of problem we ran into, while filming with Harvey Smith, was human rather than mechanical. We filmed at two locations in Spain, including a golf scene at

Sotogrande which is down on the Costa del Sol. In the locker-room sequence, while I was showering after the golf, Harvey had to pick up my bottle of Splash On and say: 'Oh, this is Brut 33 Splash On, is it?' Then he had to turn to the camera and smile.

Right. So we went through the whole scene and then Harvey picks up my Brut 33, says his words perfectly, turns to the camera and gives it a right glare, as if someone had just stolen his horse.

'Cut! Cut!'

'Er, Harvey,' says the director. 'That was a little bit serious for us. What we'd like you to do as you turn to the camera is to give a smile or a wink or something nice and friendly. Right?'

'Yes,' says Harvey.

'Take Two,' someone calls.

We go through the whole rigmarole again, and at the end of it Harvey turns to the camera. Dead serious.

They did another take. And another. And another. Harvey could *not* crack a smile. He was completely stone-faced until well after thirty takes. Then he gave a little flicker of a grin.

'Great, Harvey, great!' shouted the director. 'That's it. We've got it!'

I must be careful not to give the impression that I am the big know-it-all. I don't find smiling to order such a problem, and usually I am fairly relaxed, but that is not by any means the whole art of appearing in front of a camera.

Funny things happen whether you like it or not. I can say a sentence from the script, for instance, and get it wrong. I know it's wrong, but the mistake can stick; it somehow gets implanted in the brain, and then it's murder to try and shake it off.

Somehow the cameras or the microphone must have a kind of hypnotic effect and freeze people. I have seen good talkers – people who never seem embarrassed or short of a few words – go into a kind of trance like a rabbit in front of a snake. They can't get the words out, they can't

H FOR 'ENRY

smile or do anything.

Think of those panel games on radio which depend on people *not* being able to talk fluently once the clock starts and they are up against it. People on those games can get themselves into a hopeless twist – and most of them are professional broadcasters. I would bet, in fact, that nine out of ten inexperienced people could not think of enough things to say about their favourite hobby to make up a talk lasting as long as half a minute. And if they had a television camera on them, I bet they would freeze up after ten or fifteen seconds.

It doesn't seem to matter whether the work is scripted or ad-libbed, for the newcomer the pitfalls can be paralyzing. Somehow he or she has to get over the fact that the camera is there, or at least they have to learn to speak to it as if it's a friend. As I said earlier, most boxers are show-offs and I have never had special trouble in finding something to say. But the work I have done on TV shows – the panel games and the guest appearances – is pretty different from the commercials. There always seems to be an extra element of surprise.

In the beginning, while I was still boxing, I was appearing on programmes like *Sportsview* and *Sports Report* which were strictly about fights and other events in sport that were going on at the time. Then the idea came up for *A Question of Sport*, in which two teams compete to answer questions. I did about ten years with the programme, and it turned out to be one of those steady successes which must keep the programme planners happy because, if they didn't know anything else, at least they knew what was going to be on BBC-1 at around seven-thirty every Monday evening.

When I started out with the programme, it was presented by David Vine; Cliff Morgan was one of the team captains and I was the other. As they still do, the other two team members changed around. In the early days my big worry was that I would either dry up in mid-sentence, or the old memory would suddenly go blank when I was being asked to identify someone really easy, like Freddie Mills, say, or Bruce Woodcock. But, in fact, although I may have missed a few of those questions where you want to kick yourself afterwards, I don't think I made any real screamers.

People have asked me if I used to swot up on sports knowledge before each new series. The answer is a definite no! I reckoned that if I didn't already know something, I never would. At school I wasn't any good at swotting, and I couldn't see the point in trying to pick it up all those years later. In any case we never had even the vaguest hint about the questions we were going to be asked. The only clue that Cliff and I had was that if the guests on one team were a footballer and an athlete, and there was a cricketer and a swimmer on the other side, then the questions would probably favour those sports. But since we didn't know who was going to be on the teams until about two days before filming, it was no great advantage. Every sport has its own huge history of people, clubs, performances, records and so on, and I wouldn't have known where to start even if they'd given me the freedom of the British Museum for a month!

Certain sports definitely mean more to me than others. Athletics is one that does – and boxing, of course. I fought at the 1952 Olympics in Helsinki, and the concentrated atmosphere of those six weeks away from home helped to fix a lot of things in my memory. We lived in apartment blocks over there, and on one floor they put all the boxers. Upstairs they had the wrestlers and below us were the fencers. Another point about those Games was they had a fine bunch of competitors. In the boxing there was Floyd Patterson, Laszlo Papp of Hungary, Willee Toweel of South Africa, and Ingemar Johansson. Obviously, if any of their pictures came up later on *A Question of Sport*, I would have been well choked if I hadn't come out with the right answer.

I have also found that faces and places register more strongly with me if I first saw them when I was still relatively young. On *A Question of Sport* I was always better at identifying people from the Fifties and Sixties than from more recent times. I would be more likely to spot someone like Joe Davis or Walter Lindrum, for instance, than one of the latest snooker players. I believe that is something which happens with a lot of people, and has to do with being more impressionable in your youth, so that once a piece of information goes into your memory from that period, it seems to stick better.

The routine for the programme meant going up to Manchester every other Sunday to film two episodes at a time. The programme itself didn't cause any great problems, but we had more than our share of technical difficulties because of the video line. This was the line which supplied our pictures and it had to come from London. Whether it was because it was Sunday I am not sure, but I do know that we were forever being held up during filming and then having to wait – often for hours – while they found the fault and gave us back our pictures.

When the programmes were finished and wrapped up, then of course we had to face another trip into the unknown with British Rail – and the things that lot get up to on Sundays are unbelievable! Work on the line doesn't come into it. I reckon they must redesign the whole network every weekend.

One Sunday we thought we'd never even get there. The train limped slowly up to Manchester, stopping all over the place for no reason we could see, then crawled to within sight of the platform at Piccadilly Station and came to a grinding halt. From the train window Cliff Morgan and I could actually see the BBC people who had come to meet us, all hopping up and down and waving and giving themselves heart attacks because their precious filming time was draining away and there was nothing they could do about it. We sat there for at least an hour. It was incredible. There was no obstruction on the track, in fact we never found out what prevented them from taking us in. After an hour we had got to the stage of thinking they might as well shunt us backwards to London, then all of a sudden, jolt, jerk, bang, and we were in the station.

That fortnightly rail trip was worth a book in its own right, because something funny seemed to happen every time we went. But the strangest of all our journeys was the one with the Vanishing Waitress.

We set off from Euston as usual one Sunday morning. In the compartment with me were Cliff Morgan and two of the other sports stars who were appearing on the programme. We had been going for about ten minutes when a young girl, aged about fourteen, appeared in the doorway holding a clipboard.

'Good morning, gentlemen,' she said, all bright and cheerful. 'Would you like to order any tea or coffee, or sandwiches?'

'Oh, very nice,' we said. 'Yes please.' This was a lovely surprise, because more often than not they never even had a buffet car on this train. Now we were getting waitress service. Cliff ordered four coffees and a load of ham sandwiches. The girl looked these up on her clipboard and said it came to two pounds fifty. So we gave her three quid and told her to keep the rest for herself.

'Thank you very much,' she said. 'The buffet won't be serving for another half an hour, but then we'll bring your order round.' And off she went.

After she had gone somebody said: 'Isn't that good? Cute little kid, wasn't she, and she'll make herself a few bob doing that. Especially on a Sunday.'

We decided she must be the daughter of the guard. Anyway, the half hour went by, then it was forty minutes, then three-quarters of an hour. We were wondering where our coffees had got to when all of a sudden the guard slid back our door. With his other hand he was holding this girl (our nice waitress) by the scruff of the neck. Then he gave her a fair old push into the compartment.

'Excuse me, gentlemen,' he said. 'Has this girl taken any money off you?'

'Yes,' said Cliff. 'We've just given her three pounds for

coffees and sandwiches.'

'Right,' said the guard. 'Do you want to prosecute her?'

'Eh?' we all said.

The full story didn't come out till several weeks later. Then we found out that this sweet young enterprising girl had gone up the whole length of the train with her clipboard collecting orders and cash for teas, coffees, sandwiches, cakes, plus all kinds of drinks like beers, brandies, gin and tonics...you name it, she didn't say you couldn't have it. Then she went and locked herself in one of the toilets, put all the money into a sock, and when the train passed through a certain station she threw the sock out of the window on to the platform where her mother was waiting for it.

The guard told us some of this at the time, but we said no, we didn't want to prosecute her, so the guard took her off down the train.

H FOR 'ENRY

By now they did have a proper buffet open, and we decided to go down there and get ourselves some coffee. While we were in the buffet car, the guard turned up again with the girl. Only now, instead of being the nice friendly polite girl who had taken our orders about an hour before, now she was the loudest, most foul-mouthed little scrubber you ever saw. She was calling that guard everything under the sun. Then she broke away from him and ran up to the buffet counter.

'I wanna coffee,' she bawled at the steward.

So then the poor old guard had to run after her. 'You're not having a coffee,' he said, grabbing her by the shoulder. 'You get away from there. You're not spending the customers' money.'

She said: 'It's *my* money. I'll do what I want with it.'

'Come off it', said the guard. 'What do you mean it's *your* money. Where is it?'

'In me purse,' said the girl.

'Oh yes?' said the guard. 'Where's your purse, then?'

She gave him a real sneer. 'Up me arse.'

The poor old guard was sweating blood. He couldn't get this girl under control and she gave him terrible verbals all the way to Manchester. The only consolation for him was that she didn't wriggle away when we got there, so he was able to shove her on to the Railway Police.

Later we read a newspaper report about it, which told the whole sad story about this girl and her mother. But at the time, unless you were the guard, it did have its funny side – even though the girl was a right little monster.

Back on the television circuit, the offers of work have come in steadily over the years, and all told I must have done several hundred hours on panel games of one kind or another. *A Question of Sport* was the longest-lasting, but I have also told a few diabolical jokes on *Celebrity Squares* (not my jokes, they give them to you) and written a few daft things on cards for *Blankety Blank*.

Terry Wogan's programme is one I especially enjoy doing. There is always a good atmosphere in the studio, not only because of the hospitality, which is laid on very well, but also because now there is a regular little club of people who appear on the programme. Another good thing is that the format allows you to be yourself and put your personality across. I never know who is going to be on until I get to the studio, but there are bound to be a couple of people I have worked with before – or played golf with. In Terry's case, it's both; we have done our time up at Gleneagles with Peter Alliss, and the same goes for quite a few of the others. Or it may be that we have done things for the Variety Club or one of the showbiz charities.

    I have also been on the Morecambe and Wise show, appeared with Jimmy Tarbuck, and done a couple of chat shows as a guest of Michael Parkinson. That is another kind of programme I like because it's all ad-libbing and you can do it off the top of your head and enjoy yourself. I also did a nice sketch with dear old Tommy Cooper, who died only just recently. The situation was that Tommy was due to appear on the Ed Murrow Show and I was going to box at Madison Square Gardens. Unfortunately, the Americans got us mixed up so Tommy was sent to Madison Square Gardens and I went to the studio. Tommy was always marvellous at gags like that, with his great bear-like shape and the confusion written all over his face. Quite like a boxer, did you say? You should have seen him on this programme!

    All in all, that side of my television work has been a lot of fun. As a rule I prefer to stick to light-hearted material and not get involved in anything too heavy or serious, such as a religious programme. Although I became a Roman Catholic when I married Albina, and we practise our religion, I would not want to appear, for instance, on *Stars on Sunday*. I feel that religion is a personal matter and I would prefer not to have to push my beliefs and philosophies on to other people. Nor do I think that is what I am best suited to doing, which is also the reason why I have turned down other offers to take part in University Union debates at Oxford and Cambridge. That kind of speaking, where you have to develop an argument for or against something, is not my line and I think

*Early days on **Sportsview** – when I still had a nice head of hair!*

*In the studio for **A Question of Sport**, with presenter David Vine and Freddie Trueman.*

TAKE FIFTY-SIX

'Or you can splash it on all over.'

'What, **four** Shredded Wheats?' 'No, two.'

*Seven lovely smiles from one of the **Blankety Blank** teams. Clockwise from me are Dora Bryan, Larry Grayson, Françoise Pascal, Windsor Davies, Terry Wogan and Aimi Macdonald.*

it is best left to people whose education or work has trained them to think and present an argument systematically. I reckon there are enough professional arguers in the country already, what with all the politicians, trades union officials, journalists, etc., so if the phone rings with an offer like that I say I'm sorry but I'm not really keen.

Singing, on the other hand, is much more up my street. It was Maurice Gibb of the Bee Gees who first got me into it. One day he told me he had written a song for me.

'Go on,' I said. 'I'm no singer.'

'Yes,' he said. 'Give it a try. Surprise yourself.'

So I agreed, although I didn't think it would come to anything. Then by the time I was in the recording studio I was beginning to wonder if I wasn't going to make a right mug of myself, but somehow or other I got through it and eventually it was released. In case you have forgotten, it was called *Knock Me Down with a Feather*. It didn't get in the charts but it sold fairly well and was a nice surprise all round. It also led to another offer, this time to do an LP of old London songs like *Doing the Lambeth Walk*. It was one of those pub singalong records. Now that I already had one record under my belt, I wasn't bothered about taking this on. I was quite pleased with the result and in fact it has sold very well. Soon after it was released, a friend came to see me at home and I put the record on.

'Guess who that is,' I said to him.

'That's easy,' he said. 'Max Bygraves.'

ONE AT A TIME, LADIES

We have always kept our office staff in the family – if you include Jim Wicks, that is, who was so close to being part of the family that there was never any difference as far as I was concerned. Albina keeps the diary, as she has done for a long time now, and I do quite a lot of the business side myself. I learnt to do this when Jim went down with his final illness. By then I knew what we charged for the various jobs and so I arranged the deals direct. Now, because I am out nearly every day of the week and have to do a lot of travelling, I have agents who help to look after certain areas for me. One is a theatrical agent and he covers my personal appearances, another looks after the press side, and a third fixes up the public-speaking engagements.

The diary has become a bit of a wonder to me. When I first stopped fighting and wasn't going to the gym any more, I was naturally glad that the offers to attend lunches, open shops and so on kept coming in, but I didn't really think it would last more than five or six years and then it would start to die down. It hasn't been like that at all. In fact, this side of the work is now bigger than ever. My attitude to that is: 'Thank God.' I am not going to knock it, but I still find it strange when someone rings up with a request and names a date months ahead in the future, maybe even a year away.

'Hold on,' I say, while I look it up in the diary. 'Oh. Sorry. I can't do it. I've got something else lined up for that day.'

'What?' they say, and you can hear the disbelief. 'I'm asking about next June, not this June.'

'Yes,' I say, 'I'm sorry, but that day has gone.'

There is no great master plan to it all, but basically I have consultancies with two or three firms such as Fabergé, Valspar Paints and Cooper's Tools, and I do advertisements and in-store promotions for them. Then I fit the other personal appearances round the consultancy work.

They have quite a lot in common, because whether you are opening a new shop or helping to promote a range of goods inside a shop, you end up doing very much the same sort of thing. In the last chapter I described some of the television commercials, especially the ones with Fabergé. Also for them I have been round just about every big branch of Woolworth's, Boots and British Home Stores in the country, certainly all those in the big cities. I also do in-store promotions for Valspar Paints and plan to do the same for Cooper's. They are a big American manufacturer of hand tools and they want to move into the British market. They sent me a gold-plated hammer, and that is the tag we are planning to use – Henry's Hammer, allied to the name Cooper which we happen to share.

There aren't many secrets to making personal appearances. It's common sense really, but in the PR game you don't do yourself any favours if you look miserable or scruffy, or if you turn up late. Some years ago I had a tie-up with a car warranty firm called Autoguard, and it was while I was working for them that I learned a very important lesson: never try to do too much in one day.

This is a rule which I now apply to all the companies I work for, but it was while I was dashing round London for Autoguard, trying to fit in visits to four garages or dealerships in the same day, that I saw what a crazy game I was getting into. At that time we had daily schedules which might say, for instance: 11 o'clock, Hammersmith. 12 o'clock, Richmond. 2 o'clock, Hounslow. 3 o'clock, Feltham.

Once you have tried to work to a schedule like that, you find out, first of all, that it is impossible, and second that the people who plan it back in the office have no idea about time, and how long it takes to get from A to B in heavy traffic – let alone turning up all smiling and immaculate, going into the place, making a little speech, handing out free gifts and doing autographs for every single member of the public who comes forward.

Of course, you never know how many people will come. I have been lucky in that I get a generally good response from the public. But if it's too early in the morning, or it's a lousy day, people aren't going to turn out. On the

H FOR 'ENRY

other hand, if it's a fine day they may come in their thousands – and if they do, you've got to look after them.

Going back to that sample schedule, about the only thing we were doing right was starting off on time at Hammersmith. So far so good. Except that the sun was shining and more people had come than the organizers expected. As a result, everything took that much longer to do, especially the autographs, so we didn't get away from Hammersmith until 12.30. Then we hit the heavy lunchtime traffic so it was after 1 o'clock when we got to Richmond. Only the second call, and already we were more than an hour late.

At Richmond everyone was very kind about the delay, apart from a couple of lady shoppers who wanted me to know how long they had been waiting with their heavy baskets, pushchairs and three bored young kids. I can't blame them, but there isn't much more you can do than give a smile and a wave and get the show started as soon as possible. This one lasted until 2.45. There was no time for lunch, just a sandwich in the car while we dashed across to Hounslow, arriving there ten minutes after we should have been at Feltham which was the stop after this one. By the time we did get to Feltham it was after five o'clock, it had been raining for about twenty minutes and as I stepped out of the car an old lady aimed a swipe at me with her handbag. 'Where the 'ell 'ave you been?' she wanted to know. Behind her I caught a glimpse of myself grinning down from a poster. 'Here at 2.30. In Person,' it said underneath. Blimey, what a way to create goodwill! That day I reckoned we had drummed up more ill feeling than goodwill.

It's not just cars and road traffic that can gum up your schedule. Another time, I was flying down to the West Country to do some in-store promotions for Fabergé. We got to Northolt Airport in good time, only to be told we couldn't take off because there was thick fog at our destination, and until that cleared we were stuck. We phoned through to explain, and to say that we would be on our way just as soon as the weather improved, and would they ask the people to

ONE AT A TIME, LADIES

be patient. Even then, when there is nothing you could have done to avoid it, you still feel a little bit responsible for letting the public down. On that occasion we were more than an hour late taking off, and altogether about an hour and a half late reaching the store.

So, one way and another, that is why we changed the rules. Now, if I am on a tour of sales outlets, we do just one call in the morning and one in the afternoon. That way we are much more likely to keep the crowds happy by being punctual, plus there is time for lunch in between and, with luck, I can get my head down for a few minutes in the car while we are driving to the afternoon venue. (That, by the way, has become a standing joke with the PR people who take me round on these trips. I am the world's worst company in a car or a plane, because I can be guaranteed to be asleep within ten minutes of setting off on the journey – or two minutes if it's after lunch and I have had a glass or two of wine. I say to them: 'Look. Wake me up about a mile before we get there.' Then, zonk! I'm off.)

Inside the stores we put on all kinds of promotions, and in some ways the public never cease to amaze me. With Fabergé we had a scheme which offered a free gift to the first forty people through the door. I heard stories of women starting to queue up at four o'clock in the morning!

Then you get the professional competition entrants, who go in for every competition they hear about, in magazines, newspapers, shops, anywhere. The more practice they get, the more successful they become – way beyond just winning a few presents to give away at Christmas. The sky's the limit with these people – free holidays, cars, caravans, furniture, china – they will chase any prize you like to put up, all the way down to a free tee-shirt. People in the marketing business say they can spot these professionals by the way they fill in their forms. Often they go under an assumed name, but I suppose there is a limit to the number of different addresses they can give, and so the competition organizers find out about them that way.

In my case, if I am appearing at a store we might run a

competition to guess my weight, with the nearest guess winning a prize. Nothing enormous, but interesting enough to pull in one or two of these pot-hunters, which to my mind isn't really fair on the other people who have come along for a bit of fun, because they are now much less likely to win the prize. To me, these promotional days are meant to create a bit of goodwill all round and get people interested in the new shop or the new product. But you get a few who are real terrors. They think the whole thing is like an extra birthday party – theirs – and they compete to see how much free stuff they can pack into their trolleys.

They don't half make a noise as well. That part of it doesn't bother me because it's usually just a lot of good-humoured cackling and shouting, a bit like the atmosphere at a big fight. On the other hand, there can be other similarities with a ten-rounder at the Albert Hall, and the most important part of the organizers' work is to make sure it doesn't become too much of a bun-fight.

This means working out a routine that keeps people moving in a controlled, methodical way – they come in one door, go past the stand and out through another door. If it is just left to the customers, you are asking for trouble. They will stampede after any free gifts they can clap their eyes on, and crush anyone who gets in their way. Little kids who have been put at the front so they can see better are now getting their noses flattened against the barriers because the people at the back can't wait their turn.

Many's the time I have had to grab the microphone and try and calm things down. 'Look,' I say, 'be patient and we'll get through this much quicker than if you keep shoving and elbowing. I am here for an hour and a half and I'll do all your autographs. So, let's be having you by all means – but one at a time, ladies, *please*.'

I don't think anyone means any harm – they just get over-excited when the bright lights go on and there are prizes and free offers going. All the same, some of those people who, minutes before, were sedate housewives and dear harmless old grannies, ought to see themselves when the action starts. Compared with them, the men who come along are angels. Usually they have been brought along by their wives to do a bit of fetching and carrying, but I have noticed that a lot more men do come out shoppping nowadays, whereas before they would have said it wasn't their job or made some excuse.

In the last dozen years or so I have opened just about every kind of shop you could think of, from jewellers to DIY stores, and supermarkets by the dozen. In that time some high-street traders have taken a few heavy blows, what with the recession (now on its last legs, I hope) and the trend towards out-of-town shopping at hypermarkets and discount warehouses. But the marvellous thing is that for every hard-luck story you hear, there's always at least one new person coming up with a bright idea for a new shop or some way to make buying a little bit easier, or more enjoyable, or cheaper. I certainly wish them all well. To me, shopping is an activity that should be made as pleasant as possible for every community, whether you live in a country village or in one of those inner-city areas that someone's knocked about a bit. As an ex-greengrocer, I know it isn't easy to become the best, and to go on doing it day in and day out. It takes a lot of stamina to get up in the dark every morning and go to market. It's like a boxer doing the old road work – he wishes there was some other way of getting fit to go fifteen rounds with the world champion. He knows there isn't, so he bangs on round the streets and looks forward to a nice hot bath at the end of it.

I mentioned earlier that I prefer not to get mixed up in anything too serious, like doing religious broadcasts or taking part in university debates. At first I wasn't too sure how I would like making after-dinner speeches, because they are a good bit longer than the kind of speech you make when you open a shop. For some people I can understand that it would be a forbidding prospect, especially with all the formalities and bits of ceremony that they might not know about, so they would be doubly afraid of putting their foot in it. Fortunately, my career in boxing taught me not to be too

frightened of a bunch of guys in bow-ties and dinner-jackets, especially after they have got a good dinner inside them and the port decanters are going round the tables like batons in a relay race.

In fact, what these clubs and societies want from an after-dinner speaker is simply a bit of fun. They don't want a big lecture, and the more jokes you put in the better. So when they ask me along, they want to hear about some of the funny things that happened to me while I was boxing. That's what they know me for, and if I started bending their ears about Lloyds underwriting or something unexpected, it could all be a bit painful.

H FOR 'ENRY

Over the years I have worked out a basic routine which I can vary according to the type of occasion. It is always based on incidents from my fight career, and people can have the quickie, where I just tell a couple of stories, maybe give away some prizes and then get down, or they can have the ordinary version which lasts about twenty minutes or the longer one which goes on for about thirty-five minutes. After that, if they want any more I throw it open and we have questions and answers.

It has become quite an important line of business for me, and I am now in the fortunate position of having to ration out the number of dinners I go to as a guest speaker. If I wasn't a family man I could be out four nights a week going to these dinners. As it is, I may go to two or maybe three in one week and then do none at all the following week. The only rule I make is: never play the same place twice. I think this is sensible because if you stick basically to one routine you know you are playing to your strength. If you start varying it too much, or take on another subject you know less about, the result is bound to be less good – unless you are a brilliant actor or comedian, in which case you would be doing cabarets not dinners.

There was one date I agreed to appear at which then had me really worried. This was for the Royal Warrant Holders Association – the people who supply the Royal household – and I suddenly found myself down to talk to eleven hundred of them at a banquet at the Grosvenor House. This wasn't just a dinner-jacket job, either. All the men were expected to wear stiff collars and tail coats. In the order of speakers I was down to follow Lord Mancroft, who is a brilliant, witty speaker and a very clever man who makes it all seem so effortless. 'Blimey,' I thought. 'I can't just bung that crowd the old boxing routine.'

So I got out the encyclopedia and started scratching around for some peg to hang my talk on. I found that the first president of the Association had been a cooper, so I worked in a joke about that, and then after a bit of flannelling about I got gradually back to boxing and the old familiar territory.

ONE AT A TIME, LADIES

The combination went down very well and afterwards they said it was one of the best speeches they had had.

I do a similar kind of personal appearance plus a speech for companies. If they have a golf day, for instance, we all play in the competition during the day and then in the evening I present the prizes and give a little talk. The atmosphere is usually very relaxed by then, and what they really want is to hear some good stories and have a laugh, so I just do my best to oblige.

I have also been to a few literary lunches. They always seem to have three guest authors, and after the meal each of us has to get up and talk about our work and the book. Then we go and do the signings. This is the crunch spot. It is fine if the public want your book – but not so funny if they don't. In my experience, two of the authors would be kept busy signing away – and I have always been one of the lucky two, thank goodness – while the other one was left stranded and looking like a lemon with a pile of books which nobody wanted to buy. There's nothing you can do about it, but you do feel embarrassed for the one who's left out in the cold. It isn't necessarily their fault that they haven't caught on with that particular audience, in fact they may have made just as good a speech as anyone else. But then, when it's time for the audience to put their hands in their pockets, they have to decide. Do they really want all three books? Probably not, because they are usually about three very different subjects. So then they have to choose – and that's when it develops like the bookies' boards before a three-horse race. One is always the odds-on favourite, one is quite fancied so is marked up at about evens, but the third runner is nowhere. Suddenly that third one has become very unfashionable and all the money goes on the other two.

I hope it never happens to me. If it does, I'll know it's time to retire from literature.

CONFESSIONS OF A GOLF CELEB

I came late to golf, and that has really meant two things. First, I am probably much keener on the game now than I would be if I had started as a kid. Golf is a game for life, and I am still whacking my way round whenever I can – up to four times a week if possible – to make up for lost time.

The second point is that I came to golf too late to get really good at it. I started when I was thirty-five going on thirty-six, and at that age you can't expect to develop the grooved swing of someone who got into the game at school or college. Unless, of course, you're dead natural at it. But in my case the old muscles had been trained to do other things and were too set in their ways. As I mentioned earlier, when I was twenty-six a famous orthopaedic surgeon said that my left elbow had the wear of a man in his late seventies. So I wasn't physically ideal for golf when I took it up ten years after that.

Fortunately, this doesn't have to affect your enjoyment of the game. Golf is always competitive, whether you are trying to beat an opponent, improve your handicap (right now, mine is twelve), or just hit better practice shots. You can only do your best each time you go out. Sometimes you win and sometimes you don't. But – and this is the great joy of the game – sometimes you can win against champions.

Golf is the only game where the rules allow you to receive shots so that you can be on level terms with the guy who has just won the US Open. Then, if you are on your game and hit your shots right, you can beat him. It's almost incredible, but it's one of the unique assets of golf. You could never do that in cricket, for instance. If I took on one of my contemporaries, say Freddie Trueman, he would bowl me out straight away and so we would never have a match, no matter how much you handicapped his batting. The same thing goes for football. I could never compete with Bobby Charlton because he'd run circles round me. On the other hand, someone like that wouldn't want to get in the ring with me because I'd knock him out.

The other great joy with golf is the courses you can play. Just because you are a middling amateur doesn't mean, like with football, that you can only play in the park or somewhere in the middle of Hackney Marches along with eight hundred others. With golf you can play the pro on the same course where he won a big tournament: St Andrews, Gleneagles, Sunningdale, Wentworth ... I can play all these great courses, and many more besides. Imagine going along to Lord's, or the Melbourne Cricket Ground, and asking if you can have a game there. You'd get a right raspberry.

When I first started playing golf we were living in Wembley and I joined the Ealing Golf Club. That is still my club and the pros are still Arnold and Owen Stickley. They have been there for about thirty years and have established a great tradition. Arnold was probably the better tournament player – he won the PGA Close Championship in 1960 – but I would say that Owen is perhaps the better teacher. I'll give him a plug, anyway, because he taught me – not that I am much of an advert for him. Anyway, between them they run a very nice club. All my golf mates are there, too, so when we moved to Hendon six years ago I didn't really want to change clubs. The Hendon club is just three or four minutes from our house but I thought about the business of leaving one club, joining another and having to make a whole lot of new friends, and in the end I thought I'd stay where I was. It still only takes about a quarter of an hour down the North Circular so it's not as if it's impossible to get at.

Also, I can still go and have a lesson with Owen, who knows all about the way I play. If my game suddenly goes to pieces and I can't put it back together by myself, I go down to Ealing and ask Owen to come and have a look and tell me what I'm doing wrong.

In that respect I am extra fortunate because I play a lot of pro-am tournaments, which can put me in with the finest pros in the world. In the last Bob Hope Classic I went round with Bob Charles who is probably the best left-hander playing today. I am a leftie myself, so we had plenty to talk about. He was very forthcoming and gave me a couple of

Using a touch of science in the 1983 Bob Hope Classic at Moor Park. With me is Alan Baker, a golf mate who sometimes caddies for me.

tips about my game which I am concentrating on now. I was in a bit of trouble at the time and wasn't hitting the ball at all well. He reckoned I was squeezing the club a bit too hard and so I ought to try and relax my wrists a little. Then he said he thought I was a bit high-handed in my grip, so if I could just get the hands down a shade that would give me a smoother action with the club coming through more on the inside.

This was all good advice and I was glad to get it from someone like Bob Charles. In some ways the pro finds himself in a difficult position with the amateur, because he knows it isn't down to him to criticize the amateur's style. If you are hitting the ball reasonably well and are fairly happy with your game, most pros will leave you to get on with it. They know, after all, that you are getting lessons from someone else on a more or less regular basis, and that every teacher has a different method. So they won't try to interfere unless you are obviously suffering or you ask them.

The pro-am game has developed into quite a circuit in the last few years. I am lucky enough to be invited to play in most of the tournaments, and there is now a seasonal pattern emerging. In the early part of the year, while the British courses are wet and windy or covered in snow, we can go off to Spain for a pro-am which is held just before the Spanish Open. Jimmy Tarbuck has his Spanish Classic around that time as well, and that is always a lot of fun. Jimmy has about twenty-five teams down on the Costa del Sol, and each team consists of one celebrity and three amateurs who are put together in a draw at the first night party. Then all the teams compete over three rounds using Stableford scoring.

Later we have the Benson and Hedges, the Marley Classic, and the Harry Secombe Classic for the Lord's Taverners – which is their big fund-raising event and earns them about £30,000 each year. One that I used to enjoy was the Kenya pro-am; I played in three of those but unfortunately they don't hold it any more.

The celebs who go round the circuit are usually either from sport or showbiz. Some of the tournament regulars I can reckon to run into are Richie Benaud, Bobby Charlton, Jimmy Tarbuck, Bruce Forsyth, Kenny Lynch – and that's just for starters. It has become quite like a touring club, and I think most of us enjoy that. We certainly get a lot of laughs. It's competitive, too, because everyone likes to see his name on a cup or win one of the prizes, and this makes them a bit sensitive about each other's handicap; if they think yours is too high, you get labelled a bandit. When my handicap was higher than it is now they called me a bandit. Then I won a cup so that put me out of it and they started looking for somebody else to pick on. When Jerry Stevens won the Bob Hope Classic two years ago he was playing off a handicap of twelve, so then he was the chief bandit and they cut him to eight or nine.

The other way these games are competitive is in the side-bets. What with byes and automatic presses, if there are four guys out on the course, some of them can have about six simultaneous games going. When it comes to the reckoning-up at the end the air if thick with guys saying: 'Right. Flat on that one, minus one, flat, plus one ...' and then they are all digging in their pockets and pulling out wads of peseta notes or whatever currency they are dealing in. Spanish currency is extra popular, because with the exchange rate at over two hundred to the pound you can be talking grandly in thousands even if you have only won or lost a tenner or a score. Mind you, you need a good memory if you are going to keep track of all those little tricks and variations over eighteen holes, and a good memory is something I don't have. So I like to keep it simple with maybe a game and a bye. That means agreeing on a stake for the game itself, then you offer your opponent a bye if he loses on the game; this gives him a chance to win half his stake back. For non-golfers, the way it works in practice is: suppose you win the game at the sixteenth, you have won the main stake, which we will say is ten pounds. Then, because you have two holes left to play, you offer your opponent a bye. If he then wins the last two holes he gets five pounds back. If he loses again, he is fifteen quid down on the day.

We have had a lot of fun travelling about to the various tournaments. One journey I well remember was completely unscheduled. We all turned up at Heathrow to fly up to Scotland, only to find they had one of those sudden industrial disputes and no planes were taking off.

Dear old Graham Hill, a special mate of mine, was with us and he said that he had a plane over at Elstree and offered to fly some of us up to the tournament. 'I can get six in,' he said. Well, we all thought it would be better for the tournament organizers if some of us showed up rather than none at all, so we sorted ourselves out and six of us plus Graham jumped in a couple of taxis and shot over to Elstree.

Graham pulled his plane out of the hangar and warmed it all up, then we climbed in. There was Jimmy Tarbuck, Bobby Charlton, Dickie Henderson, me and a couple of others. We got ourselves settled down and looked around us. Those little planes look small enough when you see them from a distance parked on the airfield, but when you are sat inside, with every seat filled, they are tiny, like a Dinky Toy. We had all of us flown a good deal but this journey must have seemed a bit special because we all started grinning at each other and making silly remarks. I remember someone asked Graham how high we were going to fly and I said:

'Make it about three foot six, will you, because that's my inside-leg measurement and I can get out quick if I want to.'

Then Jimmy Tarbuck wanted to know how Graham reckoned to find his way up to Glasgow.

'No problem,' said Graham, and he held up a crumpled old map and pointed to the middle of it. 'We just follow this crease up the middle of the map until we get there.'

There's no answer to that, is there? Not when it's your pilot speaking.

Going back to the pro-am events, these have come under a certain amount of fire recently from some of the pros who are not altogether happy with the format. I think this is something the press has exaggerated, because if you really go into it you find there is only a fairly small number of objectors. Most accept that this kind of event is popular with the public and that pro-ams are a good alternative advertisement for the game of golf and its unique advantage of allowing amateurs to line up on equal terms with the best

professionals in the world. Certainly, the pros have no real grounds for complaint when it comes to prize money, since this is well up with what they can win at many events on their own exclusively pro circuit.

H FOR 'ENRY

One problem that can bother the pros is as big a source of aggravation to the amateurs: the crowds. I must be careful here, because events such as the Bob Hope Classic raise big money for deserving charities *and* depend on good and generous public support. But. The big but is that the people who go to the Bob Hope are not the same people as the golf fanatics who follow the Open on all four days (although that too is turning into a bit of a social event). Quite a lot of the spectators at pro-ams go for the golf, of course – and there is plenty of fine golf to be seen. At the same time, there is another section of the crowd – and sometimes it's the majority – who are really there for a day out and a bit of fun, with some celebrity-spotting thrown in.

The rules of how to behave on a golf course don't always get obeyed on these occasions because your casual spectator doesn't know them. It simply doesn't occur to some of them that when a golfer is in play they shouldn't move or talk. With them it's all: 'Wahey! Look, there's Jimmy Tarbuck.' 'Yeah. And what about that thing he's got on his head? Looks like a Scottish pizza to me!' 'Ha, ha, ha!'* Then: click-click-click go the cameras – exactly at the wrong moment. No wonder some of the professional players feel they are being got at. These things don't affect the amateurs so much because many of them have a sports or showbiz background and they are used to a bit of uproar while they are working. But to a pro the noise of a camera clicking can be devastating if it's done at the wrong moment. There is no harm in people taking photographs when the player is placing his ball, or after he has played his shot – but to click the shutter when the poor old pro is at the top of his backswing is not being kind to his game or his nerves.

I don't mind this background noise personally. I even enjoy it because it helps to buck me up. I think to myself: 'Here. I'd better hit this one good or I'm going to look a berk in front of several hundred people.'

There was a time when I did not feel so sure of myself. I will never forget my first pro-am, at Birkdale; I was terrified.

*Sorry, Jim, but you do wear some lovely hats.

I was playing with Kel Nagle and on the first tee my knees were shaking with fright. I had to say to myself: 'Look, come on. You've boxed at Highbury in front of forty thousand people. What do you want to get yourself into a state for up here?' This line of talk didn't do much good, because I knew very well why I was getting worked up. There may only have been a couple of hundred people watching at Birkdale, but they had come to see me (among others) do something I wasn't trained to do.

I must have hit the ball somehow and got started on the round but I can't remember the details. What I can remember is that it took some while to pick up enough confidence in my golfing ability to appear more relaxed on the tees and to start playing decent shots with some consistency.

Even so, there are some areas of the game which it is difficult for the amateur to cope with when he is playing with a pro. At the Bob Hope event, for instance, I was driving off the back tees, the same as the pros. This meant that for sixty yards out in front of me there were two solid columns of people, one on the right of the tee and one on the left. They had watched the pro drive off with no trouble, dead straight down the middle, and now it was my turn. I stepped up, and immediately I could see problems. Being a leftie, I am a little bit inclined to slice my tee shots, so I never like to see spectators coming too close down the left-hand side. I shouted to them and gave them a wave:

'Stand back a bit, will you, else you might get hit.'

They thought that was hilarious. 'Oh, yes,' they shouted back, and all had a good laugh. Nobody moved.

'No,' I shouted. 'Move back, will you. I don't want anybody to get hurt.'

Some of them started to get the message and moved back. But then the ones on the end found that they didn't have such a good view, so, just as I was addressing the ball, they all stepped back to where they had been standing. A few of them even took an extra pace forward.

In the end I had to hit the ball and luckily it wasn't a

H FOR 'ENRY

slice. But I wish some of these spectators would take a little more care of themselves. I have seen people hit on the golf course and it can be very nasty. If the ball is coming off the tee it must be travelling at a hundred miles an hour and it is bound to do damage if it strikes a spectator. I hit somebody on the wrist once, and in seconds a bruise came up which looked just as if a golf ball had been slipped in underneath the skin. Black as my boots as well, it was. The guy was going through agony – which wasn't surprising – and it was fortunate that one of the St John Ambulance people was nearby and could give him some quick first aid.

All right, so that was him taken care of – but what about me? For the rest of the round I couldn't get it out of

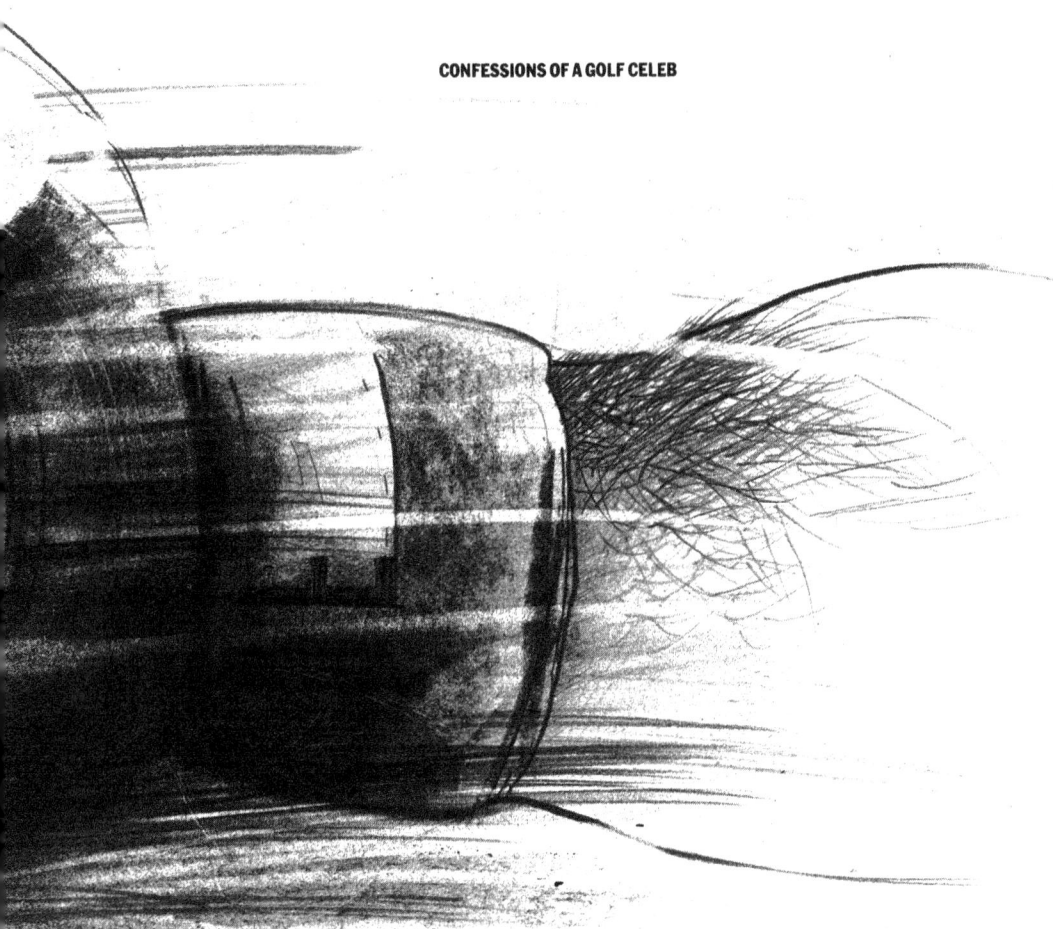

my mind that I had injured somebody, so I was really put off my game. I started holding back on shots and was only too glad to get back in the clubhouse at the end of the round.

Luckily, that time it wasn't a serious injury. As bruises go, it was a classic, but that was all (so far as I know). But I do wish the public would be more sensible when they are watching amateurs. I don't want to hurt a single soul, but I am also not a fortune-teller. I never know for certain whether my next tee shot is going to be a good one and go straight or whether I might slice it or pull it. If it's a bad shot, that ball can be as lethal as a miniature rocket. And if it's got somebody's name on it, all I can say is – don't blame me. I already told you!

CHARITY BEGINS AT HENDON

I would be the last to deny that the charities do wonderful work. I am closely involved with several, mainly through the Variety Club, the Water Rats and the Lord's Taverners, and I know for a fact that many groups of sick and handicapped people would not be nearly so well cared for if it wasn't for the equipment and buildings which have been bought for them out of charity funds. All the same, let me give you a tip-off.

If you are at a charity function, and someone gets up and starts auctioning off a pair of Henry Cooper's boxing shorts, be careful. They could well not be mine. In fact, they are probably somebody else's. I know that because I have been cleaned out of boxing shorts for years. I haven't got a single pair in the place. So, unless the ones in your auction are coming round for the second or third time, they may not be the genuine article. Of course, if you don't really mind, that's okay by me. If you just want to put them on and have a little spar with yourself in front of the bathroom mirror, you probably don't care whose shorts they are anyway – and the charity benefits whether they are mine or not.

I am not accusing anyone of flooding the charity market with fake Henry Cooper boxing shorts. I don't think the market would stand it, or that my old shorts are as interesting as, for instance, Queen Victoria's old nightdresses. They're a lot smaller, for one thing. But, just in case you want a few pointers on how to tell the difference, here you are. All my shorts were made by Lonsdale, they all carry the Lonsdale name across the centre of the belt, and they are all made of royal blue velvet with white silk side stripes and belt and my initials on one leg.

Now we have got that settled, I will tell you why I am clean out of my old gear. Each year, I get about two hundred letters from people connected with charities who don't ask me to make an actual appearance for them, but instead they ask if I can send something personal which they can auction off. I would like to oblige them all, but now I just have to send

CHARITY BEGINS AT HENDON

off a batch of signed photographs. I have already given away all the old boxing kit.

For each of my big fights Lonsdale used to make me a pair of shorts, just like I've described, and they would send them to me automatically. I have given every single pair away. I haven't even got any of my amateur gear. All the shorts and singlets have gone. So have all the gloves. When I fought Muhammad Ali for the world title, Lonsdale made me a beautifully embroidered velvet dressing-gown with Union Jacks and my name across the back. I gave that to a charity – and I am happy to say they got £2,200 for it at their auction.

Where I draw the line on giving away personal belongings is with my cups and other trophies, because they bring back very special memories for me. I can remember where and how I won each one of them and I feel they are too personal to give away. So I have hung on to them, but all the actual fighting gear has gone.

The first cup I ever won was a midget compared with some of the later ones. It was about two and a half inches high and about as wide as an egg cup. Mum cleared a special place for it on the sideboard, with nothing else round it, and every day she gave it a polish. Later, George and I were often among the prizes, so much so that by the time we were eighteen we had won about twenty canteens of cutlery. We also had the usual amateur boxer's collection of electric kettles, toasters, cake stands, trays, coffee percolators, alarm clocks... Every year at Christmas we would lay out what we had won, and any member of the family could pick out what they wanted, or, if they weren't there in person, Dad's sister decided for them. Mum, I remember, was specially pleased with an hors d'oeuvre dish shaped like a ship's wheel, and a silver butter dish. Dad's favourite was a pair of nutcrackers; every Christmas he'd get them out and say: 'Crack any nut except a coconut, these would.'

That way, all our amateur prizes that could be used for something got passed round the family. Some of them may still be in use, but most of them would be museum pieces by now – over thirty years old and fit more for the dustbin than the kitchen shelf.

Most of what I do to help raise money for charity is connected in some way with sport. Golf is the number one activity, and I am now chairman of the Variety Club Golf Society. Our main work is to organize celeb-am tournaments and find sponsors for them. Through these tournaments we raise about £100,000 to £150,000 a year for Sunshine Coaches. This is a marvellous scheme which collects money to buy coaches which carry handicapped kids about and give them holidays they would not otherwise get. Whenever we have raised the money for a new coach we buy it and then, at our next meeting, we ask representatives of the school or hospital to come along with some of the children and we present them with the keys to their coach.

The scheme was started by a wonderful old man called Leslie Macdonald who at one time was head of Moss Empires, the theatre group. When he became chairman of our Golf Society he was determined to help handicapped kids like those he had seen in the East End of London. Although some of them were eleven and twelve years old, they had never seen the sea, never been into the country, never even seen a farm animal. He reckoned that the best present he could give these deprived kids was to take them out into the sunshine. So he started this scheme to buy coaches and take the children out of the cities and into the fresh air where they could see things for the first time in their lives. A cow in a field may seem a bit ordinary to you or me, but Leslie Macdonald uncovered something far more important – that hundreds of handicapped kids had spent all their lives missing out on some of those things which are so simple that ordinary, healthy, mobile people take them for granted.

Sunshine Coaches began some fifteen or sixteen years ago, and now operates all over the UK and in some foreign countries, including Kenya. In the Golf Society we are very proud of the fact that our tournaments have raised enough money to put more than seven hundred coaches on the road.

H FOR 'ENRY

Raising the money is not always easy, especially nowadays when finances are leaner than they were a few years back. But all our members are generous people, whether they are from sport or showbiz or have an ordinary business background. They need to be generous or there is no point in them belonging to our Golf Society, which exists to raise money for charity. Everyone who is invited to become a member must be prepared to put up a couple of grand a year or so to help with the sponsorships. At one time it used to be possible to find one person or organization who would put up £25,000 or £30,000 in one go and that would be enough to get one entire tournament off the ground. Today it is more likely that we will split the main sponsorship round two or three people or companies who each come in for £8,000 or £10,000. Or we can do it by asking people to sponsor one hole each for £1,000, which raises £18,000. Then somebody else might offer a special prize for a hole in one, and we build up the charity's take in small lots. As chairman of the Variety Club Golf Society I am there mainly as a front man, while others who are more expert at it than me go out and gee up the sponsors. We have our committee meetings as well, of course, where we do our planning and discuss policy. You get one or two disputes every now and then, but I don't need a hammer to bang on the table. I just say: 'Right, that's it. We'll do it this way.' I'm big enough, and they don't argue.

The Lord's Taverners is another charitable organization which I have belonged to for many years. They support various charities, such as cancer relief and the one to help people suffering from muscular dystrophy, and when I go in with them it is mainly to appear at dinners and play in their golf tournaments. A lot of the members are famous cricketers, or keen fans of cricket, and I have also played in some of their charity matches.

I have dropped that out a little bit lately because, to be honest, I was never any good at it. A lot of the other guys were ex-county cricketers, even England internationals like Denis Compton and Trevor Bailey, so I was always on a hiding to nothing on the cricket field. They knew that, of course, so they used to stick me out on the boundary to keep me out of the way. Always, though, someone on the other team had to go and bash a skier in my direction. Out there in the deep there is no hope that one of the good players will come sprinting up and shout: 'Mine!' Out there in the deep it's always: 'Yours, Henry!' So I'm running about under the ball, backwards and forwards, waiting for it to come down. Even when I was still fighting I was playing in these cricket matches, so then I'd be thinking: 'Blimey, if I don't catch this right I could break a finger and have to pull out of the fight!' Nine times out of ten, I had so many things going through my mind to distract me, I'd miss the ball completely or drop it. 'Aaaah!' goes the crowd. 'Oh, bad luck, Henry!' go my teammates, all with big sporting grins on their faces. Later they give you terrible hassle back in the pavilion, and you find out they are worse than golfers. They want to win all the time, these guys. At cricket? I ask you. 'Leave it out,' I used to tell them. 'How can you want to win so much if you put me in your team?'

    Batting wasn't much easier. I am a left-hander and I always thought my stance was beautiful. I'd go out to the crease, take guard and shape up to the first ball with a lovely straight bat, all copybook stuff. Then the ball came down and everything went all over the place. It didn't matter if it was fast or slow, a full toss, a wide, straight, a long hop – whatever the bowler served up, I had to have a dirty great slash at it. If the ball was straight, I would be bowled first ball. If the ball was wide of the stumps and I connected, I would still be out first ball because then it would loop up in the air and give someone a dolly catch. Alongside the other celebs or showbiz people who played for the Lord's Taverners – people like Eric Morecambe, Brian Rix, Leslie Crowther, Tim Rice, Ronnie Corbett – I was a middle-order disgrace, so nowadays I am giving cricket a rest.

    Still, we had some good afternoons down in the country, playing against the village teams. We raised a fair amount for charities, too. These matches are usually played on a Sunday and so we could not charge admission. Instead, the money was raised by selling programmes and by taking a blanket collection. I've done a few of those – the long walk round the boundary asking people to throw money into a sheet or a blanket which you are holding with somebody else. People always respond very well to these appeals, chucking in pound notes and 50p pieces so that on a nice sunny afternoon you can raise three or four hundred quid. Then all the celebs do their stint in an autograph booth, and that also does a lot of good. I have sat in a tent signing autographs for half an hour or so and enough people have come in during that time to bring in thirty or forty quid for the charity.

Another event which has given me a lot of pleasure is the 'Henry Cooper's Walkabout' at the White City. This is for the Variety Club, and the idea there is that they send out an appeal which says: 'Come and do fifteen rounds with Henry Cooper.' Luckily for me, I don't have to fight them all; the 'fifteen rounds' means fifteen laps of the White City Stadium. People get their friends and relatives and neighbours to sponsor them and then what they have to do is get themselves down to Shepherd's Bush and walk round the track fifteen times. We have done the Walkabout for three years, and from the latest one we raised £40,000. This was a very nice increase on the year before, when we pulled in £30,000, so naturally we are very grateful to the public for all the support they give us.

All sorts of organizations help us – Scouts, Guides, Cubs, commercial companies and clubs – as well as private individuals. A friend of mine went round people she knew until she had collected £1,000 worth of sponsors, and the wife of another friend organized about fifty girls and between them they raised £7,000. To me that seems an incredible sum for, basically, one ordinary private person's effort and inspiration.

Talking about effort, I am trying to pace myself. A golf invitation, as I have said before, is something I will always try to fit in if the diary can take it. Eating dinners and talking

CHARITY BEGINS AT HENDON

A bouquet and a giggle for Joanne Kingdon, the winning nurse in the Miss St John Ambulance competition of 1977.

A knees-up for two, skipping to raise money for Help the Aged. With me is Lillian Fieldman, the organizer of the charity.

Now get out of this! Ronnie Corbett is in a bad lie on the floor of the Savoy Hotel after a Variety Club lunch. His opponents are myself, Dickie Henderson, Bruce Forsyth and Max Bygraves.

On the march with Lulu for the NSPCC.

afterwards – that is also something I can still handle. It's the physical stunts I am not so keen on – what you might call the Superstars bit. Don't think me rude, but if you asked me to push a wheelbarrow from Lambeth to Land's End for charity, I could well end up telling you about my bad leg. I *have* done a couple of 'It's A Knockout' contests for the Lord's Taverners, but I reckon that is my lot. I *have* been asked to run in the London Marathon. It didn't take me long to say no, either. I just thought about Kenny Lynch and what happened to him. He ran a London Marathon, pounded round the streets for twenty-six-odd miles, got to Westminster, finished. Great. Well done, Kenny. Afterwards, his knees and ankles swelled up so much he could hardly walk for a week. The way I see it, if I tried to do that I wouldn't be able to play any golf for a month. I don't fancy that, so I have to be hard and say no. Also, there is my age to think of.

A couple of weeks ago I was fifty. Not only that, my brother George was fifty as well – although when George got to fifty I was fifty years and twenty minutes. Anyway, to prove we had got the count right, the Variety Club threw a marvellous party called 'Henry Cooper's Fiftieth' at the Hilton Hotel. It was wonderful to be honoured in this way and perhaps now in this book I can take the opportunity to thank the organizers again, and all the guests and the people who made speeches and did the cabaret, and tell them what a smashing do it was.

The party was held in the evening, and then a few nights later the cabaret and speeches were shown on television – so I've got that bit on video as well. Harry Carpenter was the compere, and this is how he began it:

'My lords, ladies and gentlemen. Welcome to an evening of heavyweights. In the red strip, celebrating his fiftieth birthday, Mr George Cooper. Mr George Cooper is preparing to meet another fifty year-old, Mr Henry Cooper, Knight of St Gregory and an Officer of the British Empire.'

They started with some good old cockney acts. First, Chas and Dave sang a song about me and Ali, where there was a bloke with all the lip, and another bloke who said he'd 'put the Lip to kip'. Then, from the Players' Theatre company, we had a bit of *Knock 'em in the Old Kent Road, Boiled Beef and Carrots, Old Iron* and some of the other favourites which, for me and George, are part of our earliest memories of growing up in Camberwell and on the Bellingham estate.

Then Harry Carpenter came back and explained some of the aims of the Variety Club and its fund-raising efforts. This was mainly for the TV audience because I think everyone present in the ballroom knew that part of the story. Then Harry switched to the work of the Variety Club Golf Society and brought on a series of celebrity guests, starting with Tom O'Connor who made a very funny and, to me, moving speech. (It's a good thing they have those big white napkins at the Hilton, so you can give yourself a mop-down when the talk gets a bit personal).

Next to come on were the Flying Pickets, all dressed up in shiny boxing outfits, and they gave us *When You're Young and In Love.* Then Bobby Charlton came on and thanked Albina and me for inviting him and Norma to the party. 'I think it was a good idea, Albina,' he said, looking round at the hundreds of faces, 'that you didn't try to have it at home.' That fetched a good laugh. Then he said some things about my golf handicap which I won't go into, except to say that *he* thinks I dropped it by a couple of shots only after *he* resorted to physical violence...

When Harry Carpenter took the microphone again, he paid a very nice tribute to my great old manager, Jim Wicks. It's funny how the same remark or characteristic sticks in different people's minds, but in an earlier chapter in this book, called 'Adventures With The Bishop', which was written several weeks before the Hilton party, I remembered how Jim and I always referred to ourselves or each other as 'we', and got ourselves labelled as 'the weeing couple'. In Harry's story about this habit of ours, he told us how he interviewed Jim one weekend after I had lost a fight through getting cut badly when I was ahead on points.

'Pity about Henry getting hurt like that after he had been going so well,' said Harry to Jim in the studio.

H FOR 'ENRY

'Yerss,' replied Jim in that heavy wheezing way he talked (and which Harry imitated to a T). 'Well. You know. We was going along quite nicely, until – unfortunately – *our* eye got cut.'

'Jim always spoke with the Royal We,' said Harry. Then he brought on a right trio of lads – three of the commentators who, like Harry himself, had followed some or all of my boxing career from the ringside. They were Desmond Lynam, Reg Gutteridge and Eamonn Andrews, and they all paid me some lovely tributes which it would be embarrassing for me to recall here – especially Eamonn's which was in verse! Anyway, I remember that Reggie got a big hand when he put in a word for 'the lovely Italian bantamweight, Albina'.

Then we had what for me was the treat of the whole day. Harry called into the audience and summoned up 'the three times heavyweight champion of the world – Muhammad Ali!' I can't honestly say I didn't know he was there, and the television cameras had not been able to resist a quick focus on him a few minutes earlier. But what I felt was so good about it was that Ali had accepted the invitation and flown over from Los Angeles for the party knowing full well that it would be like putting his head into an opponent's training camp. There at the Hilton he would run into a very British audience – the cream of our showbiz people, sportsmen and commentators, all celebrating *my* birthday and recalling the big moments from *my* career. At least two of those big moments had to do with Ali, sure, and he could always be secure in the knowledge that he had won both of our fights. All the same, what this audience really wanted to see and cheer about was the time when I knocked him over with the left hook in the fourth round at Wembley in 1963. They had seen it on film, it had been in Chas and Dave's song at the beginning of the cabaret, Eamonn had it in his poem… and now good old Ali was coming up to be interviewed about it. People had been going on about what a nice man I was, and saying all those kind things about my work for charity – but I reckon that in Ali the audience were looking at one of the most remarkable men they were ever likely to see in person in their whole lifetime.

He is slower now, and he doesn't speak with the old sharpness. But there is still that glint in the eye, and the confidence that goes with knowing you are one of the all-time greats of sport.

Ali sat on a big sofa on the stage opposite Harry Carpenter, who said to him: 'You have been as close to Henry Cooper as most people. What do you most remember about him?'

'He hits hard,' said Ali. And when everybody had finished cheering, he went on: 'I tell people, it's a funny thing, but Henry hit me so hard, he jarred my kinfolks in Africa.' More laughs and cheering, then Ali said: 'I was really so lucky, because as soon as he hit me the bell rung, and I had time to recuperate.'

'Otherwise?' Harry asked him. 'What would have happened otherwise?'

Ali took a dive sideways into the arm of the sofa: 'Zzzz.'

H FOR 'ENRY

When Ali stepped down, the cabaret whirled into action again. Harry had found out that one of the favourite people I like to listen to on my cassette player when I am travelling around in my car is Stéphane Grappelly. So they tracked him down to New York and from there he sent a special birthday message and played one of his great tunes, which he fronted with a slow waltz-time version of *Happy Birthday To You*. Then Patti Boulaye came on and sang a nice serenade about my face. Well, it didn't sound like the one I see first thing in the morning, but if Patti wants to flatter me I'm the last one who's going to complain.

She was followed by a couple of outside broadcasts from three of my friends from golf. Peter Alliss was down at the Berkshire course with Jimmy Tarbuck, filming an episode of *Around With Alliss*. Jimmy was wearing a kind of topless hat with a visor, and he and Peter had a few chirpy things to say, including some diabolical statements about their ages. As Harry put it when they were off the screen: 'Peter Alliss has got about as much chance of seeing fifty again as I have.' Then he went on to explain that the next guest was 'hoping shortly to celebrate his thirtieth birthday'. Well, they must have got that link completely wrong, because the next face to come up was Terry Wogan's! He certainly didn't have the nerve to come right out in person and *say* he was twenty-nine. In fact he didn't even mention the question of how old he was. Instead he started attacking me, accusing me of 'always being fifty'. Blooming cheek. I expect that's why he filmed his piece in a recording studio, because he knew that if he'd said that to my face in the Hilton, I'd have stepped over and clipped him one.

Anyway, next thing, Harry Carpenter got us all calmed down and announced that Prince Philip, the Duke of Edinburgh, had sent me a birthday message. He invited Norman Garrett, Chief Barker of the Variety Club, to read it. This was a marvellous honour for me, of course, as if I hadn't been honoured enough that day. The message contained a very fine and generous tribute to me, which I will never forget. It also recorded the Duke's personal thanks for the work of the Variety Club in raising money for youth charities, and in particular for the special Awards scheme which carries the Duke of Edinburgh's own name.

When he had read the Duke's message, Norman Garrett went on to say just how much this year's fund-raising meant in pounds, shillings and pence, all of which went to help sick and needy children and other worthy causes. Then Norman called me up on the stage and made me a presentation of a beautiful engraved silver salver. Now it was down to me to contribute something in return.

Well, how do you begin to thank all the people who have come to an occasion like that? Norman had already said there were seven hundred people sat down in the ballroom, and I explained that we would be there all night if I tried to thank every familiar face. However, on behalf of myself and my brother George, I began by thanking Trevor Ching, who had generously sponsored the whole birthday party. Then it had to be just a very short list of thank-yous. I gave my thanks to Albina, bless her heart, and to our old Dad who was there in the audience. He is 84 now, so I just asked him to stand up and show his face. That's just the sort of invitation he likes, so I had to tell him to sit down again quick before he started to give us a speech of his own – which he is well capable of, I can assure you. Then I specially thanked Muhammad Ali for coming over all the way from Los Angeles, and told him – in case he'd forgotten – that when he was fighting he was the greatest thing on two legs. I don't think he has forgotten, mind you, because he just gave a quiet little smile while the whole room burst out with a big storm of applause.

Finally, I thanked my brother George and hauled him up on stage to join me and let all the people see us together. Two peas in a pod, we once were, although in our business you get your features altered a bit over the years. Still, even these days, we can just about get away with the identical twin trick for a couple of minutes – or as long as it takes to eat two Shredded Wheats!

I have many reasons to thank George. In the

beginning, at the Lying-In Hospital in York Road, Westminster, on the Third of May 1934, I was only born because George was there to help push me out and I arrived in the world twenty minutes before he did. Then for twenty-six years we were constantly together, at school, in the Army, and in boxing. We each started out with our own fight careers, and then George retired but he didn't quit the game. He started his own business as a plastering contractor and then, in the last three or four years of my career, whenever I had a fight he would let others take care of the business for three or four weeks while he came to help me and be my trainer. He was a ready-made sparring partner as well. In fact he helped out in a dozen important ways. We always went away during that time and George and I lived together for twenty-four hours a day, just like we had done in Bellingham. When I got up in the morning to do the road work, George was there on the bike; after training, he gave me a rubdown, and we would spend the whole day together. Then, on the big night, he was always in my corner. So, although he has always stood back a little while I have been in the limelight, I know that without George and his encouragement I would not have achieved half the things I have managed to do.

After I had said some of that and given my thanks to everybody, Harry Carpenter took charge again and introduced a great bunch of kids from two boys' clubs in Islington and Grove Park who brought on a huge cake and sang *Happy Birthday To You*. Then we had *Knees-up, Mother Brown*, and with that song we came to the end of the greatest party of my life. Or nearly to the end.

The reason why it wasn't completely over was that we still had another presentation to make, just across the road. This was a sort of return match, because now it was our pleasure to go to Buckingham Palace and present the Duke of Edinburgh with a cheque for his Awards scheme which had been raised as part of my birthday celebrations. We all went into his private study and he asked how the party had gone. I told him a little bit about it and how Muhammad Ali had come over from Los Angeles, and then I presented the cheque. The Duke's reaction was to say that he thought *he* should be giving *me* something – which I thought well summed up the attitude and kindness of someone who has done as much as the Duke of Edinburgh has for charitable causes.

That ceremony over, tired but happy, it was time to go back to Hendon and duck out of sight for a bit. Not for long, though. I may be fifty, but if I want to get a personal message from the Queen as well as from her husband, I'd better keep myself fit – because that won't be coming through the letterbox until the Third of May 2034.

THE FIGHT REPORT

In his career as a manager Jim Wicks went from running a squad of fighters to looking after just one man – me. When I retired, Jim was happy to pack it in also. At the time, though, I remember thinking – and saying so in several press interviews – that it would be nice if I could find one really promising young heavyweight and train and manage him myself.

I may have been wrong about that. It might not have worked out quite so rosy as you tend to picture things when you first start looking at them. In any case it never happened, and now it is very unlikely that it ever will. In 1971 I had plenty of PR and advertising work to keep me occupied, and the momentum of keeping to all those dates and deadlines, plus the extra ones that were coming in, meant that the boxing project was put to one side and didn't really progress beyond the stage of being an 'interesting idea'.

Another small but slightly important point is that, just as you don't walk down the street and find a lot of nuggets of gold lying on the pavement, you don't come across too many good heavyweight prospects. In 1971 I could not see a single fighter coming up in the sport who looked as if in three or four years' time he could really make the grade. So, over the months, the other work took over and I no longer had the time to offer someone if they had come along. What is more, I would have been fooling myself if I had thought I could train and manage a boxer part-time, squeezed in with all the other jobs. It is definitely a full-time job in its own right, and the fact is I was too heavily involved with other things to get disentangled from all of them and make a 'comeback' into boxing. Today I have got bookings in my diary for a year ahead, so now it would be even less possible to take it on.

It is a shame in a way, because there are some good fighters around. Terry Lawless has proved that with his stable – a group very much in the style of what Jim Wicks once had. As usual, there are not a lot of outstanding

THE FIGHT REPORT

heavyweights coming up (and that is the weight I am still most interested in) although Frank Bruno has got to be rated a good prospect. Of course, as people have been saying for some time, he needs better opponents now or he will stop being the big draw he has become. At the same time, his manager has got to pace it all very carefully. We saw in the fight against Jumbo Cummings how vulnerable Bruno can be to the sudden swing that gets through, so they have got to do a lot to tighten up his defence. At the moment he is a bit exposed on his left-hand side, and also he needs to get his right hand up more so he can use it to fend off punches and guard his chin.

On the more positive side, the Cummings fight showed that Bruno could take a good dig and come back afterwards. When he was hit with that punch, he was out on his feet and if he had gone down he would not have beaten the count. I think he was lucky in a way, but it is one of those almost freak things that happen in boxing. If a fighter gets a dig on the chin, his nervous reaction may vary. One kind of reaction is to make the legs go stiff. That is what happened with Bruno, his legs went rigid and propped him up while his brain was still working out what had happened and what he ought to do next. With the more usual kind of nervous reaction – provided the punch is hard enough and timed right – the legs will crumple, and in that case the fighter is lucky if he comes round in time to beat the count. Ten seconds is a very short time when that is all you have in which to recover from the blow, sort yourself out, get back on your feet and convince the referee that you are fit to continue. In the Bruno–Cummings fight, there were only a few seconds to the bell, and Bruno managed to stick it out on his feet until the end of the round. As soon as the bell did go, Lawless jumped in there and pulled his boy back to the corner to start working on him.

Bruno proved in that fight that he had his share of bottle. He took the blow, and then he came back and won. A lot of fighters in that position would have got swamped in the next round – if they had managed to come out for it. So

H FOR 'ENRY

that was a good sign, and now if Bruno can tighten up his defence and learn to stand a little less rigidly, he could have a very good career ahead of him. (I certainly hope that by the time this book is published, nothing will have happened to make these remarks out of date.)

Correction! It already has. Just two weeks before this book went off to the printer, Frank Bruno got himself knocked out in the tenth and final round against James 'Bonecrusher' Smith, and the whole future of our best heavyweight prospect has to be looked at again.

I say 'got himself knocked out' because that is just what he did. He allowed it to happen. Until Smith tagged him in the last round, Bruno was heading for a win on points. All he had to do was pace it right and he would have been home. Then, when he got caught, he didn't show that instinct for survival which every boxer must have. He wasn't out on his feet, like he was against Cummings, so he should have 'claimed' his opponent, as we say, which means he should have grabbed him and hung on to him, playing for time and seeing out the round. Or he could have gone down and taken a long count, then got up when his head was a bit clearer and hung on until the bell.

What worries me most about this performance is that Bruno didn't know what to do. He was up against the ropes with his hands down, and did nothing to save himself. That worries me more than the fact that he was obviously knackered anyway for the last two rounds. His big left jab was more of a paw, and it seemed to me that all his heavy arm and shoulder muscle was working against him. Big, bulgy muscles like that burn a lot of energy and a lot of oxygen, and from round nine onwards he could hardly raise his fists to use them. If he was *that* tired – and we know he wasn't used to going ten rounds – it was tactically wrong for him to keep coming forward like he did. After the fight Smith said: 'Bruno made the mistake of trying to take me out instead of tying me up.' Which only supports what I am saying.

I don't want to knock the guy because he's had one

THE FIGHT REPORT

defeat. But his manager, Terry Lawless, was so upset by the result that he threatened to quit the game. I don't want to knock Terry Lawless either, after all the things that he has achieved for his fighters. But it has to be said that if I had been in Bruno's position at the end of round nine, my old manager would have been telling me: 'Right. You've got the fight. Don't get involved. Get on your bike and keep moving. Go backwards, go away from him. Don't take chances.'

Still, there we are. Maybe the Bonecrusher Smith fight was a blessing in disguise. It showed that Bruno was not ready for the really big opposition, and it will do him a lot of good to have four or five basic learning fights and work his way back. If he had beaten Smith, they might have put him in against Mike Weaver, and that could have been a disaster. He might not just have got hit, he could have been injured. Now, at least, Bruno has the chance to learn more about defence, and how to pace himself and move about the ring, before he gets stuck in with one of the big world-class guns.

That Sunday night at Wembley was a double sickener for Lawless, because he also saw his other big hope, Mark Kaylor, get floored five times by another American, Buster Drayton, before the referee stopped the fight. In Kaylor's case, I feel he was more unfortunate than Bruno. When you have two big hitters in the ring, you can never be sure who is going to land the first heavy blow which turns the fight. I was caught a few times in my career, and I think this was one of those bad nights which Kaylor will have to live with every now and then. He is still a good prospect, but at the time of writing we shall have to wait and see what happens when he fights Tony Sibson for the European middleweight title.

Sunday 13 May 1984 has to go down as a bad day for British boxing, but not necessarily a tragic one. If you look at it from the promoters' point of view, it could well seem a nightmare, what with their million-dollar paydays being set back by at least a year. But we'll just have to hope that it is no more than a temporary setback, and that these two boys will come good again.

One British fighter who has been very close to the top

H FOR 'ENRY

is Colin Jones. He is the type of fighter you can never discount. Jones is a good banger, well able to come from nowhere and finish a fight with one blow. In two contests against Kirkland Laing he showed us what he can do. In both he was a long way behind on points, then Laing maybe got a bit too casual and dropped his hands and – wham – Jones caught him with the punch that turned the fight.

The problem with Colin is that he starts too slowly. This showed in his last world title fight, against McCrory. Because he likes to attack a lot, and would never reckon himself much of a stylist, he will always tend to fall behind on points. That doesn't have to be a problem, because there is the chance that eventually he will connect with a good one. But at world level it must be a risky way to plan a title fight. Against McCrory, Colin took a good four rounds to get warmed up, and by that time his opponent was well into his stride. He was much taller than Colin and had a much longer reach, and once he had got his rhythm it was never going to be easy to knock him out of it. Colin's best hope with a man like that was to get in and press him from the first bell – even if it meant doing a couple of rounds of shadow boxing in the dressing room to get himself really warmed up before he went into the ring. If he had done that, he must have improved his chances.

But that's boxing for you. It must be the greatest 'if only' sport of them all. if only I'd gone in early, if only my lucky shorts hadn't got lost in the laundry, if only he hadn't caught me with his head... There must be as many 'if onlys' in boxing as there are stones in a graveyard; a big graveyard.

Boxing itself is still in a healthy enough state, even if a lot has changed since my days in the ring. I still see a lot of fights through the various dinner shows at the Sporting Clubs, and in the work I do for BBC Radio making inter-round comments at the big title events. The main differences seem to have happened because of television.

There is no doubt that a programme like *Sportsnight*, with Harry Carpenter presenting it, has found a growing number of viewers who want to see boxing. On *Grandstand*

THE FIGHT REPORT

and *World of Sport*, too, they show a lot of recordings of big fights on Saturday afternoons. That is fine, but here is another boxer's 'if only': if only the people who enjoy watching the boxing on television would get themselves down to see a live fight, what a difference *that* would make.

Inside the halls the atmosphere is usually good, but it never really boils up like it used to. If you take someone like Charlie Magri, there is a fighter with a fierce, all-action style, and the fast-talking personality to go with it. In the old days he would have packed them in as soon as he had got within sniffing distance of the world title. But when he fought Cedeno, just a few months back, the hall was only half full. When you watch a fight like that on television you don't get a chance to notice the empty rows, but the fighters only have to look up and they are staring them in the face.

Why should the viewer worry anyway? The promoters still put on a good show, it's noisy and colourful with all the old razzamatazz like Solomons used to put on at Harringay. You still get the old champs climbing into the ring to take a bow – including me, only I have to tear off the BBC headphones first, then leap up there and dive back again into the commentary position. We get a good reception and I have always enjoyed doing it. All the same, there's no disguising the fact – if you are there – that the halls have got an echo to them that wasn't there a few years ago.

I don't say it's the public's fault. The public seem just as keen on boxing even if there is less of it around. What has changed is the way it is presented. Nowadays a promoter's big concern is not so much to fill the venue itself with fans. He knows there is always a solid core of spectators who will want to see a fight live, and that they will buy tickets for it and turn up and shout their heads off. Meanwhile the attractive money, the stuff that makes profits, is earned through closed-circuit television, through piping the big fights into cinemas. As I see it, it's fine to be making that extra money, but not so good that it's being made at the expense of the live event.

At Wembley arena, for instance, they have not had a

Pipe-dreaming about the good old days, when fighters learned their trade and built up a following down at the local baths.

THE FIGHT REPORT

sell-out since I fought Billy Walker, and that was back in 1967. Billy had not long turned pro, he was the new face, a young blond blood-and-guts hitter who didn't care if he had to take two blows to get in one of his own. That is the kind of heavyweight the public has always loved to see because you can guarantee there will be fireworks whichever way the fight goes. On a night like that, the traffic would be so heavy going to Wembley that I could be jammed up for half an hour if I didn't get in ahead of the main rush. Today, getting to Wembley is a doddle. I know there won't be any big holdups – certainly not any caused by people battling to get to the fight – so I can leave home as late as seven o'clock, drive there, park the car, stroll inside, and before seven-thirty I'm in my seat.

As a live spectacle boxing has moved a bit up-market in the last few years. Dinner shows at big hotels, for which the audience have paid a good few quid to eat well and then sit back and watch the fights – that is where the live entertainment is going on, whereas in my day the usual venue for an up-and-coming fighter was the town hall or the baths. Those old places may have been a bit on the primitive side, but they served a very useful purpose in their time because they were first and foremost *local* venues where a young fighter could start to build a following. Nowadays, if a boy is promising he will get drawn into the dinner-show circuit and that is a good thing in that the conditions and the setting are better for him as well as for the customers. The trouble is, the boy is now getting his experience in front of the members of a club, in other words they are broadly speaking the same people, and not in front of different crowds at those town hall evenings, or down at the baths, where he could have the chance to enlarge his following, so that by the time he was a contender for the British championship he would have boxed live in front of thousands of people. A lot of those people would then be keen to buy tickets and travel up to Wembley to see him on his big night.

Those small local bills have not disappeared

H FOR 'ENRY

completely, but you won't find nearly so many as you used to. Nor has the fighter with the big following disappeared. Tony Sibson, for instance, has shown that you don't have to be a Londoner to attract the right people and get good fights. As for his fans, they mostly come from his home base – around Leicester – and are as loyal and enthusiastic as a crowd of football fans. In fact, I could think of a few football clubs who might be only too glad to chuck their own supporters in exchange for a trainload of Sibson's.

Another big difference is that the fighter's route to the top has been changed. Once it was a step-by-step progression to becoming British champion. When he fought for the British title he might also win the Commonwealth (the old Empire crown), and then he would build up via the European championship to becoming a world contender. That is all out the window now, because matches are made not so much through the ratings system, which gives all the fighters a more or less even chance to make their way up the ladder, but through the eyes of the promoter. And what the promoter is looking for is big pay-days. As a result, you can get a position where people may not know who the British champion is – their attention has been drawn away to some other fight which has nothing to do with championships, but all to do with pulling in the punters and filling newspaper columns.

Just now, the British heavyweight fight that the public wants to see is Bugner v Bruno – a fight between two men with not a single title between them. Bugner has been British champion, of course, and then later he lost it. Bruno, on the other hand, is still an up-and-coming boy but, because of the way things are arranged nowadays, he may bypass the whole process.

This is something I regret because it represents the standards of a different world. When I turned pro, my greatest ambition was to hold the Lonsdale Belt which you get for defending your title successfully, and which you could keep if you defended it three times. I won three Belts outright, which you can't do now because the rules have

THE FIGHT REPORT

*In the ring with some of the lads from the **Golden Belt** series.*

been changed. Nevertheless the Lonsdale Belt remains, to me, the greatest boxing trophy of all – not just in Britain but in the world.

All that might seem old-fashioned to the youngsters I now see hammering it out for another Belt in front of the cameras of Channel 4. For the ones who do eventually make it through the amateur ranks, and don't get too interested in girls on the way, the big ambition will no doubt be to take on the world. Over the last decade they have seen a good crop of British boys get up there and grab hold of the supreme title, and you can't blame the youngsters for thinking that is what the fight game is really all about.

For the time being, these lads who battle for their home town on the *Henry Cooper's Golden Belt* series have a long way to go before they need worry too much about big-time stardom. The next step for them will be to do well in the ABA championships. It is always a big move up from the junior class to the senior, because it usually happens around the time when a boy is leaving school and looking for a job. Once he gets himself fixed up and starts earning a few quid, he finds there are a lot of other things he can do with his evenings. So it is really only the very keen ones who will get far at senior level.

At the moment I am also a little bit concerned about the standard of boxing which you see at the ABA finals. In recent years I have seen lads in there whose style was getting on for diabolical. It made me think: 'Blimey. In the old days he wouldn't have been fighting for the ABA title – he wouldn't even have been picked for South-East London.'

How do they get there? Well, again I can only think it is because boxing styles have evolved so rapidly in the last decade that we are now in a completely different phase from the methods that were taught and followed when I was boxing. Like most people, I tend to think that the methods I was taught were good and made sense, and I am not going to change my mind about any new ones until I see some really outstanding youngsters who convince me that this new phase is here to stay for some time and is worth supporting.

Physically the boys can't be very different, and the motivation is much the same. If we were living in boom years, then the numbers of young boxers might be down, but we have just been through a bad patch economically and I reckon there is no shortage of boys coming forward who see boxing as the way to lever themselves into a better place in the world. What a lot of these boys need is a new trainer.

Nine out of ten of the trainers I listen to now have one message for their boys: 'Go forward.' Go forward and pressure him, go for his head and you will win – this seems to be the sum total of their message, the only key to success. As a result, a whole lot of the arts of boxing are in danger of going extinct. None of the trainers, or very few of them, even considers a strategy that uses body-punching. They are all head hunters. 'Left hand, right hand, left hand. Head, head, chin.' That's all they say. It's a very rare sight now to see a boy who has been taught to bring his opponent on to him, then hook him to the body.

To me that is one of the essential skills of boxing. A good body punch saps an opponent's strength and can cause just as much trouble, if not more, than a punch to the head. Another thing: the body is much easier to hit. As a target, a boxer's body must be a good three times bigger than his head, but all these modern trainers want is for

THE FIGHT REPORT

their boy to keep throwing punches at his opponent's head, which is not only small but bobbing about all the time. The body, meanwhile, is much less mobile but they don't bother to go for it. It's another age. I used to concentrate on getting my opponents in the body. A few good hooks down there, one solid one in the liver – that's what brings their hands down – and then you can hit them on the chin to finish it.

The referees aren't much help. All you hear from them is 'Break! Break!' as soon as two boys get together. Consequently they never get a chance to practise any body punching, assuming they know how to go about it. This again is a by-product of the modern 'pushing forward' style of boxing, which produces many more eye injuries through clashes of heads than you used to get – and this is mainly what the referees, especially in amateur boxing, are anxious to prevent.

Some of these fighters, and their trainers, would do well to watch a few of their performances on video. Then they might see what is going on. They might even get to wondering whether it is really necessary to lead with their heads, because that is what they do. Fighters nowadays are so crouched forward that if you drew a line down from their chin, it would hit the floor in front of their feet. Now, where's the sense in that? It's about as clever as an army sending its generals in to lead the charge, with the troops following on behind.

In my family we have never had anybody who fought all crouched up, and I hope we never will. The chances are against it anyway because my sons are more interested in motor racing and my brother George's boys do karate. So George and I may be the last of the fighting Coopers, and I am quite happy to look back and think that at least we retired when boxing was still a sport which you carried out in a more or less vertical position.

Our Dad also did his bit in the ring, and once when he was in the Army reached the final of two welterweight brigade championships. I say 'once' because – typical Army –

he had to fight them both on the same evening. He won the first all right, but then found himself up against a professional in the second and couldn't make it a double. That was between the wars, and Dad's style would not have been very different from ours: in other words, he stood fairly upright. For a bigger contrast you had to go back another generation – to Grandad George.

Grandad George, Dad's father, was a middleweight who did most of his fighting in the backyards of pubs around South London. I never even met him, let alone saw him fight – all that was in the 1880s and the 1890s – but I guess he would not have been so very different from the old champions whose photographs you may have seen. The point I am getting at is that those lads used to stick their bare-knuckle fists up in front of them and lean *backwards* with their heads and bodies. When you think about it, boxers have changed their stance so much over the last century that their heads are now pointing forwards at about ten o'clock where my grandfather reckoned that one o'clock would suit him nicely. Well, Grandad and his mates may look old-fashioned to the modern fighter, but I will say one thing for the old boys – at least they could see where they were going!

ME AND MY ITALIANS

In an earlier chapter I mentioned a few moments in the life of the Cooper family, as George and I grew up in South London with Mum and Dad. Now I have a second family – the Genepris.

Albina's parents, Giuseppe and Maria Genepri, still live on the farm in the foothills of the Apennines which Albina left as a child to join her aunt in London. She was never a great one for mucking about with farm animals, and she was glad of the chance to move to a big city, even if it was hundreds of miles from home and in a foreign country. She went to school here, first to the Notre Dame de France School in Leicester Square, and then to St Peter's and St Paul's School in Amwell Street, Clerkenwell. When she left at fifteen she had a go at dressmaking but didn't like it, and her Aunt Maria suggested she came into the family restaurant business. Peter Rizzi, Aunt Maria's husband, owned Peter Mario's in Gerrard Street, and so Albina started to work as a waitress, learning to serve all the restaurant's Soho regulars, which included a few people from the fight game such as Jim Wicks – and myself. It took a little while to sink in that I liked her and she liked me, but then I asked her out and we began to see each other regularly, and about a year later we decided to get married. And that is how I also got to know Boccacci.

Boccacci is a little village about twenty miles from Parma in the north-central part of Italy, about halfway along the motorway between Milan and Bologna. That is where Albina was brought up and where her parents still live. We go over to see them regularly each year, or more often if we can. They are getting on a bit now but they still keep the farmhouse going and I have been able to help them do it up so they are probably more comfortable now than they were in the old days.

When Albina was there as a child her parents had all sorts of farm animals, but now the cows, the sheep and the pigs have gone, and her mother just keeps a few chickens and looks after her vegetable garden. They used to grow wheat and make all their own bread, and make wine from their own grapes, but fields of wheat and vines take a lot of looking after and so now they get their bread from the village and each year the old man goes and gets in a stock of grapes. He still makes all his own wine, and puts down about fifteen hundred to two thousand bottles. He still likes a drop for himself, of course, and he also likes to save up some of his best stuff for the family when they go to visit him. We all give it a good bashing, so that makes everybody happy.

Although I have been going over to Italy for about twenty-five years I still have problems with the language. I must know several hundred words by now but it's the grammar that gets me. I can't put that together and, unfortunately, Italy is one place where you have got to be careful how you address people. You can say 'tu' to people you know well or who are part of the family, but if you don't know them so well, or they belong to the older generation, you are meant to say 'lei' or 'ella' which is the polite third-person form of address. If you don't remember, or can't get the words right, they may take it as an insult. I wouldn't like to say how many people I have offended because I don't know my way round the grammar book. After a while I began to think: 'Blimey, I can't do this,' and when Albina is around I become the typical lazy Englishman. She does the interpreting and I just nod and give them a nice smile.

Henry Marco, my older boy, is much better at Italian than me. He learnt it as a child because we used to send him over to Boccacci for several weeks at a time in the summer holidays. He would run around and mix in with the kids in the village and so he became fluent at quite an early age. Even now, he's only got to be back there for about an hour and he's picked it all up again. This is going back a dozen years or so, but in those days we used to take him over there at the beginning of the summer holidays and then he would spend about six weeks living with his grandparents. Albina has two brothers who work as chefs in London, and they also went over there for their holidays, so usually one of them could bring Henry Marco back with him.

ME AND MY ITALIANS

H FOR 'ENRY

One of the treats of a trip to Italy is going out to the restaurants. For me, Italian cooking is even better than French. I may be a little bit biased, of course, but there isn't much argument that it was the Florentines who taught the French to cook in the first place, and in the Parma region where we go the people eat very well indeed. Parma ham and Parmesan cheese are famous throughout the world, and in the local town, Salsomaggiore, there are some marvellous restaurants. It's a spa town, and a lot of people go there for the baths and the water cures. I go there for the food. I have been to a lot of places in the world, and that has meant eating in a lot of different restaurants, but I would match somewhere like Il Tartufo (The Truffle) in Salsomaggiore with anywhere you could name. They have food there which is out of this world. They do a butterfly ravioli which they fill with spinach, or you can have slices of cured venison, which they cure in just the same way as the Parma ham and serve very thinly sliced. I like to eat that with a fresh pear, or you can have it with fresh figs, which is how Albina likes it. Or there's the fettuccine… I get hungry just thinking about it.

Back in my childhood days we always ate well. We were a poor family, and there was never any really decent money coming in until George and I started earning in the ring. Also, we had the war hammering round our ears for at least five of those years, followed by the Austerity period which lasted into the Fifties and meant that some kids never even saw some so-called 'luxury' foods which nowadays everyone takes for granted. Even so, our Mum was a really good cook who could make a meal out of anything. On some days she had to, if she didn't get to the top of the queue before the shop sold out, but even then she could come up with dishes that I can remember to this day. Bread pudding, date pudding, shinbone soup – the names may not make your mouth water, but somehow Mum always kept us Coopers well filled up and healthy.

Over in Italy, at around the same time, the Genepris had a few problems of their own, what with the Germans retreating slowly into the north of the country and bombers flying low over the fields around Boccacci. Albina's family knew how to live off the land, of course. That was their whole background, and the thing they did best. But they had to suffer many shortages as well as having to look after their own skins in what, after 1943, was an occupied country. For Albina's parents the problem was not so much keeping body and soul together in the food sense, but keeping out of trouble with whoever was in charge in their district.

The penalty for helping the British or Americans was death. Most of the people in the village were on the side of the Allies, especially the Genepris. Albina's Aunt Maria, the old man's sister, had married Peter Rizzi before the war and they were already settled in England, so you can imagine there was a lot of tension in the family just through having relatives living in an Allied country while they were stuck with a mixture of Italian Fascist and German rulers.

At one time the village was sheltering two British soldiers who had escaped while behind enemy lines. One of them, a captain called Peter, was in Albina's house when a messenger rushed up and warned them that soldiers had arrived in the village and were searching all the houses. Albina's father took Peter into a room where he had a special hideout. He pulled out a high-backed bench which was up against a wall, and behind it was a chimney. He pushed Peter in there, told him to keep quiet (as if he needed telling), then he slid the bench across and went out to wait for the soldiers. They soon arrived, and they searched every room - all the bedrooms, the cellar, the stables, everywhere. They must have looked under every piece of furniture in the place - but they didn't find the chimney. Peter got away and later, more than twenty years later, he returned to the village to meet the people who had helped him. He still couldn't speak much Italian, or so they say - and I'm not one to talk about that - but the point is that he hadn't forgotten them, and they all remembered him.

The community feeling among the Italians in London is just as strong. We belong to a club in Clerkenwell, the Mazzini Garibaldi, where a lot of Italians meet to gossip and

keep in touch with each other and the news from back home. Each year they organize a big outing, called a *scampagnata*. They all drive out in family parties to the country and have a big picnic with games and races for the kids. It's all well organized, and the day begins with Mass in a great big marquee. Then we get the picnic gear out, and start filling ourselves up with lovely Italian sausage, meat balls, crispy bread and cheese, and maybe one of those nice tarts or sweets the Italians make. This is washed down with a few bottles of Chianti, so then we all doze off for a bit, and after the siesta we get the kids lined up for their sports. In between there is bound to be some singing – all the old favourites from Naples and everywhere else, because there are people on the outing from every part of Italy and so they all chip in with something special from their own region.

ME AND MY ITALIANS

I enjoy it because it is all so relaxed. Sometimes in England I think we tend as a race to get a bit too tensed up and take ourselves too seriously. The Italians have their temperamental side, of course, but generally the problems blow away as quickly as they arrive. Which way is better? I wouldn't like to answer that, because everybody is born a certain way, with a certain nature and a certain background, and they don't usually step very far out of that pattern. I know I definitely wouldn't want to try and change into a different person living a different life. All the same, I do enjoy being mixed up with Italy and the Italians. As I said, I haven't quite conquered the language yet, but I'm doing all right with the food.

WALKING THE DOG

I still keep myself fit. Not like a health fanatic, or one of those people whose ambition seems to be to win *Superstars* and die. Twenty-seven years of road work and gym work are enough to last anybody, I reckon. There's always the golf, too, which keeps me out in the open air for about four hours at a time and gives me a four-mile walk into the bargain – on a bad day it's more like six miles. I like to swim as well, so long as the weather's decent and somebody's run the hot tap for a bit. Then there's the dog-walking.

I have always loved dogs, and the present one, a Kerry Blue terrier called Benson, is number three in the line. In between there have been gaps, and times when we have just lost a pet and said: 'Right. No more animals. Never again. Finish.' Then we'd get another one.

When I was a kid in Bellingham we had a nice old mongrel called Pat. She was a cross between a smooth-coated fox terrier and a whippet, and we had her all through the war years and she went on until she was thirteen.

Albina isn't all that keen on animals. Even though she comes from a farm background, as a child she always preferred doing jobs round the house to dealing with the animals – and that was one of the reasons why she was glad to come to London and join her aunt's family and live in a big city. When we got married I managed to persuade her to try having a family pet, and we got a Doberman. That was when we were in Wembley. Unfortunately he got a skin disease when he was only about fourteen months old and we had to have him put down.

'OK,' said Albina. 'That's it. We will never have another animal.'

For a while there were no pets in the house, then John, our younger boy, got to work on his Mum and she agreed to have a cat. When I heard about this I wanted a Siamese, and we bought this beautiful cat which we called Gatsby. He stayed with us for three years, then one night we let him out in the garden as usual, and never saw him again. Whether someone grabbed him, or he had an accident, we'll never know.

'OK,' said Albina. 'Now we will definitely not have another animal. Never.'

It took John a bit longer the next time, but in the end he managed to talk his Mum into letting us have a dog. So along came Benson, and I hope he's going to be a bit luckier.

The idea of having a Kerry Blue came originally from Jim Wicks. All his life he was in either boxing or racing. In the Twenties and Thirties he had a spell running Wandsworth dog track for C. B. Parks. This was an unlicensed track, which meant that he had to go to Ireland to buy his greyhounds. And Ireland, of course, is the home of the Kerry Blue.

Jim was over in Ireland and he had just bought a batch of greyhounds from a breeder when this bloke turned to him and said: 'Do you want a good guard dog, Jim?'

Jim thought about that for a bit and then he decided he quite liked the idea. A guard dog could come in very handy, especially now he was looking after all those greyhounds, which cost a fair bit even in those days. So Jim said yes and this farmer-breeder told him: 'I've just the one for you, Jim.' He vanished into some sheds and came back with a sturdy-looking dog, not very tall but solid, and with a short curly black coat.

'This is what you want, Jim,' said the feller.

'Right,' said Jim, looking it over and giving it a pat. 'Lovely.'

It was a nice-looking animal, quite friendly towards him, and Jim took it home feeling well pleased. He hadn't heard about Kerry Blues.

About a week later, the complaints started coming in. Jim had neighbours knocking on the door and telling him: 'Your dog's bit my dog.' Another one said: 'Your dog's killed my cat.' A third one said: 'Your dog's killed my dog.'

What no-one had warned Jim about was that in Ireland they bred these Kerry Blues as fighting dogs. Just as people in England once reared bull-terriers to fight, this breed was the Irish equivalent. Of course, by that time it was too late to re-

H FOR 'ENRY

train the dog so Jim had to take out a special insurance policy to cover his costs every time someone in his district came round with more bad news.

Jim put up with it for about a year, but by then he was so fed up he did exactly what the old farmer in Ireland had done to him. A guy came to the track to buy some dogs and Jim said to him: 'Do you want a good guard dog?'

The guy looked interested, so Jim went and fetched the Kerry Blue and showed it to him. 'Marvellous guard dog, that,' said Jim. 'If you had a dog like that, no-one would ever come on your land.'

The guy looked the dog over and said: 'All right. I'll have him.'

So off they went. Later Jim said to me: 'I hope he didn't have a field full of sheep, because that dog would have killed every bleeding one of them!'

Years later, once we had decided to get a new dog for the family, I was going through an encyclopaedia with the boys to see which breeds we liked, and there in the Terriers section was this black curly-coated dog. Underneath the picture the caption read: 'Kerry Blue'.

'That's the one!' I said. 'That's what Jim Wicks had.'

We found out about breeders and went to see a lady who showed Benson to us. She assured us that her dogs were not like the wild Irish ones but had been bred to have a pleasant temperament and to get on well as family pets. We took him with us, and so far he's been a success and has fitted in very well. His teeth are getting a bit sharp, mind, and if he gets excited he sometimes forgets he's meant to be steady and obedient. Then it's more a case of 'One word from me, and he does what he likes.'

Time will tell if he's a villain or not. Meanwhile, it's nice to have a dog about the house.

WHAT NEXT?

Things are always changing – like with the boxing chapter, 'The Fight Report', which needed some last-minute treatment to keep it as up to date as possible – but the latest news from home is that we are all still fit and enjoying ourselves. We have no plans to move house, but if we did I am sure the word would get round the Post Office quick enough. They would find us even if we forgot to tell them. The way some of the letters are addressed, it's a wonder they even get past the first sorting office, but they do. Envelopes come here marked 'Henry Cooper, Ex-boxer, London'. Sometimes they don't even say 'London', but the mail always gets through.

I try to see that everyone gets an answer, even the odd one or two that I could have done without in the first place. The other day someone wrote in to say that he had fallen on hard times, in fact he was so badly off, he hadn't been on holiday for ten years. He followed this up with a few more instalments of the usual sob story, then he wondered if I could see my way to letting him have £5,000 so he could go on holiday. I thought to myself: 'Blimey, why doesn't he take his wife, and then I could send him £10,000?'

Just now the weather is up and down, beautiful and sunny one day and torrential rain the next, but officially it is summer and the big rush to make films and personal appearances is over until the autumn. I have just finished another commercial for Shredded Wheat – the one where I say the lines in verse and the packets all have stickers of sports stars in them. That was hard work for someone with a memory like mine, but the company seem happy with the result.

I have a couple of appearances for Brut booked into my diary, but Fabergé have been taken over by a big American group, McGregors, and they may decide to change the image for the product; we shall have to wait and see. McGregors also make golf clubs, so I'm trying to figure out if that could be a line to develop!

What with the Shredded Wheat ads, Choosy cat food,

WHAT NEXT?

Cooper's Tools and New Horizon stationery for Spicers – a range of 'new heavyweight' brown envelopes – it has been a funny old mixture of products this year – and long may that continue. On television, the two *Golden Belt* series have gone down very well and it looks as if that will run to a third next year. There may also be a new series of *Be Your Own Boss*, the business programme.

Only the other day I was working on a couple of the new-look *Blankety Blank* programmes, which have Les Dawson as compere in place of Terry Wogan. I am sure he will get the hang of it eventually, but there was a lot of chin-pulling and desperate ad-libbing when I was there. That kind of thing sometimes vanishes in the editing, but some of this was so funny I hope they keep it in. Les and I, by the way, are Brother Water Rats, so we have had one or two good evenings together.

The golf season is well under way, and I am looking forward to doing a Pro-Celeb at Turnberry, where the pros will be Johnny Miller and Nick Faldo. I always enjoy those, whether we play at Turnberry or Gleneagles, but over on the Ayrshire coast I don't mind hoping the weather will be kind, especially on the Ailsa course when you are playing with the sea almost under your feet and the waves are crashing against the rocks by the lighthouse. Slice one there (if you're left-handed) and your ball could fetch up in Ireland.

During the summer the Variety Club Golf Society has fifteen or sixteen tournaments to raise money for charity. Last weekend, for a change, we went to Berlin to play the British Army in aid of their Benevolent Fund. We played on the British and the American courses, and afterwards we had a gala dinner at the Kempinski Hotel.

West Berlin came as a bit of a shock when I got there. I hadn't really thought about it before the trip, but when we arrived I realized that the last time I had set foot in Berlin was thirty-one years ago! I nearly had a fit to think of all that time passing so quick. Not that I recognized anything. When I last saw Berlin there was still plenty of rubble about from the war and they had an awful lot of building to do. Now, of course,

*Sticking up for **Be Your Own Boss**, one of my latest TV shows.*

WHAT NEXT?

the city is not only transformed, it is beautiful. They've got lovely avenues with trees, lakes, yachting marinas, golf courses... In the West, that is. I reckon the British, French and Americans captured the most attractive part of the city in 1945, or at least the part with the most potential. East Berlin, with its business and big industrial sections, still looks fairly like it did then – a dump.

We have another traditional golf fixture with the Army: Variety Club versus the Generals. The golf is played on one of the Surrey or Hampshire courses in the Aldershot-Camberley area. This year we played at the North Hants club in Fleet. My partner and I were drawn against a general and a lieutenant-colonel, and they did us up in style. (Crafty bunch, those Army officers, they're a lot more useful than they sometimes look.) Afterwards, everyone goes back to the military academy at Sandhurst for dinner in the Indian Room, which is a beautiful place to spend an evening in good company. I couldn't actually stay for the dinner this year because I had to rush off for another charity do, but I have been there in previous years and enjoyed myself a lot. For a tournament like that, the Variety Club raises money through its sponsors and we are then able to hand over £1,000 to the Army Benevolent Fund.

Nowadays we are so busy during the summer months, we have changed our holiday timetable and don't really reckon to get away until the winter. That suits me fine, because if the weather is good I reckon you can't beat Britain in summer. There are so many beautiful places to see – not to mention over two thousand golf courses – that you would have to be a full-time tourist to get round them all.

In February, it's a little bit different, and then I don't mind going off to find the sun. Albina and I have been over to Barbados, which is great, and I am also a director of a time-share company, Gulf Leisure, which has properties in Spain and Portugal. The one I mainly go to is at Aloha, near Marbella on the Costa del Sol. Marbella is a big golfing centre, in fact one of the biggest in Europe, and the Portuguese development, at Penina, is pretty popular too. The golf course

WHAT NEXT?

there was designed some years ago by Henry Cotton.

Back at home, Gulf Leisure have another development at Broome Park, Canterbury, which used to be Lord Kitchener's house. This is a marvellous place, full of history and on the estate there is, guess what, an eighteen-hole golf course! Not only that, the house has been converted to make fourteen or fifteen beautiful apartments, and in the grounds they have squash courts and tennis courts, and there is a swimming pool, saunas, and a gymnasium if you want a workout – I stay clear of that! One way and another, though, you'd find it hard to be bored down there.

From all I have been saying, you will see that I spend a lot of the time on the move. If I am doing a store promotion, it could be anywhere from Glasgow to Plymouth, and then my next booking may be in East Anglia or the Midlands. If it's a long-distance trip, I prefer to fly, so if the date is in Newcastle or Scotland I will drive down to the airport and jump on the shuttle. Beyond a certain distance it definitely pays to fly, both because of the time you save and because it is a lot less tiring than going by road. With the long-distance trips there is also the perk that people drive me round to the various places while I am up there.

Even with all that free transport, I still reckon to drive a good 25,000 miles a year. Where we live, in Hendon, it's only a couple of minutes to the M1, so I can be up at the National Exhibition Centre in Birmingham in an hour and a half, and we do a lot of fairs and trade shows up there. I have always enjoyed my cars anyway, so I don't mind doing a return trip like that. Mind you, I do like a bit of comfort. When you are six foot two you don't want to sit all crunched up in a Dinky Toy, so I've got to admit I prefer a car where I can stretch out a bit. If that means getting a Rolls Royce, well, that's exactly where I am at the moment.

It's a funny thing how parts of your life seem to turn round in circles, but the last time I had a Rolls Royce was when I fought Ali for the world championship. The other night he popped up again at my fiftieth birthday party, and now I find I'm asking the Rolls garage, where my son Henry Marco

WHAT NEXT?

works, to look out for another one, It will have to be second-hand, but they tell me there's a good chance and they are keeping their eyes open for me.

Looking back, I have always liked nice cars. Even when I could only run to a second-hand Ford Prefect, back in the Fifties, I was watching out for something a bit more special. My first new car was a two-tone green Morris Cowley, then I bought a Morris Oxford, then a Fiat 1800. Next was a sporty little Alfa Romeo GT – and things began to look up. I changed it for an Alfa GTI, moved on to a Mark II Jaguar, then a Mark X, then a 220SE coupé Mercedes, then a 280 Mercedes, then a T series Bentley. I never wanted to keep any car for very long, and mostly I tried to change makes or move up the range, to make the next model more interesting than the one before. Somewhere in there it was 1966, and I had the Rolls. I had a Jensen Interceptor, a couple of Ford Grenada Ghias, then a Ferrari. At present, until they find me a nice Roller, I am very happy with a Saab 900 turbo. That's a good runner and I will keep it anyway, for the time being.

The Ferrari was a special experience. It was one of the bigger models, the 365GBT four-seater, with twelve cylinders and about six great big carburrettors on it. It was a marvellous car for the open road; went like the clappers. In London, in traffic, it was another story. I wish in a way I had kept it in the garage and just used it as a fun car, because that is really what it's for. The trouble was, I was using it to go around in central London, and it was inevitable that we would get stuck in traffic. Next thing, up comes a smell of petrol and the engine cuts out because the carburrettors have flooded.

Then I have to wait twenty minutes until it has all evaporated and I can start up again. Meanwhile I'm stuck at the lights and getting verbals through the window from every taxi driver who goes past, plus a few others:

'Ere, Enery, why don't you get a decent car?'

'Blow this,' I thought to myself, choking on everybody else's exhaust fumes. 'Next time I'm going respectable.'

That was just over a year ago. Out went the Ferrari and in came the Saab, which has done me very well. But now I

At home in Hendon: Albina and me with, on the left, Henry Marco holding Benson, and, on the right, John Pietro keeping an eye on Benson.

WHAT NEXT?

have got the itch for a change, and whenever I think about it the sign that comes up in front of my eyes says 'Rolls Royce'. I don't know why. Maybe it's for the prestige, and because they really are the best. Maybe it was the magic of seeing Ali again. You can't always tell with boxers.

Illustrators

David Smith
The Man Who Gave Up Russian Dancing;
One At A Time, Ladies; Walking The Dog

David Hughes
Taking Stock; Confessions Of A Golf Celeb

John Ireland
Adventures With The Bishop;
Charity Begins At Hendon; What Next?

Richard Willson
The Fight Report; Me And My Italians
Take Fifty-Six

Picture Acknowledgments

BBC Photos 60 both, 62
Leslie Baker, Welbeck Photography 61 bottom
Birmingham Post & Mail 41 bottom
Dave Cannon, Allsport Photographic 76
Central Press 43, 93 bottom left
Channel 4 111
Daily Mirror 12
Fox Photos 28, 93 top left
Richard Garrett 61 top
Keystone Press 41 top, 93 top right and bottom right
Mark Westwood 134
Yorkshire Television 128

www.ingramcontent.com/pod-product-compliance
Lightning Source LLC
Chambersburg PA
CBHW080443110426
42743CB00016B/3257